STRANGE PLACES, SIMPLE TRUTHS

Dr Meares is a psychiatrist in Melbourne, Australia, and is the author of eleven books and more than fifty scientific papers on different aspects of psychiatry. He is a past president of the International Society for Clinical and Experimental Hypnosis. He has travelled widely, and in this book he brings us psychiatric insights into the hidden meaning of ancient customs which add a new dimension to the experience of travel.

AINSLIE MEARES, M.D., D.P.M.

Strange Places, Simple Truths

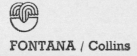

FONTANA / Collins

First published by Souvenir Press Ltd. 1969
First issued in Fontana Books 1973

© Copyright 1969 Ainslie Meares

Printed in Great Britain
Collins Clear-Type Press London and Glasgow

CONTENTS

PREFACE

Many of my friends have suggested that I should write a book on my travels. I have been loath to do this. My travels have always seemed very personal to me, and my meetings with strange people even more so. I certainly never travelled with any intention of using my adventures to write a book.

The purpose of my travels was simply to contact people such as yogis, Buddhist priests, Zen masters, witch-doctors, fire-walkers and others who have experience of unusual states of consciousness. It was my hope that contact with such people might give me better understanding of the state of the mind in hypnosis, and so lead me to improve my treatment of patients with tension and pain. You will see that this hope has to a great extent been realized. Such is the story of this little book.

You will understand that any account of such experiences must of necessity concern my own intimate feelings about these matters. I mention this only to ask your forbearance at the way in which I bring so much of myself into what I write of these distant places.

AINSLIE MEARES

March, 1969.

INTRODUCTION

An executive makes a business trip to London or Detroit or Osaka or wherever it might be. He judges the success or otherwise of the trip by what he brings back in new ideas about his business. So it is with me, only I am a psychiatrist; and my business is trying to understand just a little better how the mind works.

To see an Indian mystic transfixed like stone in his trance is an experience which is interesting in itself. So it is to watch a fire-walker dance unconcerned and unharmed on the burning embers; or to sit with a witch-doctor as he throws the bones to unravel the mysteries of bewitchment. But the real interest in such experiences is something quite different. It is the way in which they throw light on the functions of the mind, of my own mind and the mind of my patients. This is the part of my travels which I prize so highly, and which I wish to describe to you.

First let me explain how it all began. As I have said, I am a psychiatrist. I do a lot of work with hypnosis. A few years ago I was using hypnosis to help patients in pain, very bad pain, pain from cancer which could not be relieved by drugs. While trying to learn as much as I could of the way in which our mind can control our body, the thought came to me that eastern mystics are reputed to be able to control pain by meditation and yoga practice. So I decided to go to the East to try to discover for myself whether in fact this were true; and if so, whether there was any possibility of adapting some of the eastern practices to modern medicine.

I have been fortunate; and since my first venture with the yogis, I have made a number of overseas trips from Australia to give lectures or attend medical meetings in America and Europe. Each time I go, I break my journey for a few weeks in some out of the way place, and see what I can of local customs that might have some bearing on psychiatry. This has led me to many interesting insights into the way our mind works. This is what I want to tell you about.

And the purpose of it all! You may well ask, 'Was the purpose of my travels fulfilled?' The answer is unequivocally, 'Yes'.

I have learned something of the eastern approach to calm of mind and control of pain which can in fact be adapted to western psychiatry and modern consulting room practice. I have set out these principles in my book, *Relief without Drugs*. Now every day I receive letters from people in many countries of the world saying that they have gained relief from practice of the mental exercises I describe. This is my reward. It is also proof of what I say, 'that it is not too difficult to extract the essentials of eastern mysticism, and to use them to control tension and pain in a way that is consistent with the full and active life of western society.' And now I shall tell you something of my experiences of strange places and simple truths which made this possible.

To Those Who Travel

Travel! Strange places! There would seem to be magic in it, so that the idea has some kind of universal appeal. Yet when some travellers return they tell us such different tales. We can see this among our friends. Even if they only go to London, some tell us of the Abbey and Tower Bridge; others of the shops in Bond Street; others of the theatres; and others of the night life of Soho. For many a traveller these things are sufficient. But it is for you, who would seek more of this, that I write.

You visit the Taj Mahal. You breathe in the beauty of it; you know when it was built and why; but beyond all this there is meaning and inspiration. Take this home and then you have travelled.

There is yogi, statuesque in his meditation, a superb photo! Yes, of course, you understand it; he has given up our way of life for another way. But there is more, so very much more. As you see him there, just sense the meaning of it all. And the strange gods that we see when we travel! But what do we see? A bizarre creation of the heathen mind, or the dramatic expression of some aspect of the personality that lies deep within us all? And the simple things too. That peasant woman. Good if you could capture the expression of her eyes in a photo. She has learned to cope with life, a different life from ours; to have her children, to suffer, to die, and all without the help of a doctor. And of course the expression of her eyes is different from ours. We see too the odd things, the decoration of the mosque, the fortune-telling sticks in the temple, the folded paper in the Shinto shrine, the pornographic figures of the Himalayan temples. They are not just things to be gaped at. Can we bring home with us the meaning, and the inspiration of it, and so come to transcend the pattern of our ordinary living?

But there is more than this. We have touched only upon the intellectual understanding of what we see around us when we travel. There is more. Of that I am quite sure, and I hope that I may be able to lead you to something of it. There are the photographs, the souvenirs and the trinkets. This is one level. Then there is the knowledge and the understanding that comes of looking deeply into strange places and the people that live there. This is another level. But this other matter of which I speak, is something beyond this. It is the experience of it. Not the experience of going places, for that is a triviality, but the experience of something deeply personal. It is the moment when something in the peasant's eyes halts us, and somehow we understand better; or the rhythm of the girl as she dances and we see in it the eternal rhythm of all things; or the priest beating his gong and calling upon strange gods, and the strangeness goes deep because we are part of it too. These are the high peaks of travel. It is here that we momentarily exceed the ordinary limits of our being. Hidden places within us are lighted. We are illumined. But there is really nothing to photograph and very little to describe. We can describe factual events and rational feelings. But these experiences are of our inner being. They come to us when we travel in strange places as it is then that we are momentarily freed from the mundane reality of our ordinary living and the terrible constrictions it imposes upon us. In these moments something happens within us. There is a move towards a better integration of our personality, and as travellers we return enriched by something within ourselves.

1 BURMA

A Yogi in Rangoon

When viewed realistically, the whole venture seemed a rather crazy idea. I was aware of this, particularly so as I am a conservative person and in the main live an orthodox way of life. But working with patients in severe pain is quite a harrowing experience for the doctor, and I was driven on by the idea that I might learn something from eastern mysticism which might help me in the clinical use of hypnosis. So I set off in that state of expectancy which comes upon us when we are in high hopes, and when we embark on some enterprise which is rather contrary to our usual way of doing things.

India seemed the obvious place to go. I found that I could take a plane from Australia which stopped at Rangoon. So I decided to break my journey there.

While the plane was still a great way off, I caught sight of something glistening in the sun. Then as we came nearer, I could see that it was a golden pagoda. The Shwe Dagon! The great centre of Hinayana Buddhism. Here it was shining with golden light. I am not ordinarily given to omens, but at the sight of it I filled with anticipation.

But nothing glistened in Rangoon itself. The hotel was sad. All things are sad when they reflect only the glories of the past. It was dirty and falling into disrepair; yet the walls spoke of great things that had happened there in the days of the white sahib. But those days have gone for ever. Things are different now. Piles of garbage littered the main street, and the rats showed little concern as I walked past.

I found an English-speaking guide. He smiled when I asked if he could take me to a yogi. However, he said he knew of a strange man who lived amid the rubble of a bombed area of the city. We went there; and I sent the guide to tell him that I was a doctor who was interested in the control of pain, and wished that I might speak with him. He followed the guide back to me where I waited at the side of the road. He was a big man; and the longest beard I have ever seen reached down to his knees. He was calm. This was the outstanding impression that he gave. It was not perhaps so much that he was calm, but rather the great depth of his calmness. The skin of his forehead was smoothed out, and so was the skin at the side of his eyes. Most noticeable of all was the way in which he blinked. He blinked slowly. The upper lids would just descend slowly and leisurely like a curtain, and then lift again. It seemed that there was some inner tranquillity which was quite beyond the noise of the street and the squalor of his surroundings.

He could speak no English so the guide acted as interpreter. He said that he could control pain, and this was done by meditation. When others were in pain, they could be helped by breathing on the painful area. He said that he was quite free from all tensions and anxiety. This of course was merely a repetition in words of the idea already so clearly communicated by his manner and appearance. Passers-by began to gather around us. Soon I was the centre of a gaping crowd of twenty or thirty people. The kind of conversation which I wanted became impossible. He told me he was eighty years of age. I thanked him and said good-bye, and tried to give him some money for his trouble, but he refused this. In doing so I remember that he was neither pleased nor offended. There was no emotion. This was my first experience of non-attachment. In those days I had not come to understand its significance.

Next morning I bought a small bunch of bananas, and went with my guide to the rubble-covered space where the yogi lived. He accepted the few bananas and invited me to sit down by the tangled pieces of galvanized iron which were his home. We were far enough from the road to be spared the curious throng of people who had gathered around us on the previous day.

I soon became aware of another attribute of this strange man. In a way he had great dignity. I am sure he was unaware of this. It is hard to think of a man dressed in rags sitting in a yard of rubble as dignified. But this was the case. It was some product of his inner being rather than his outer bearing. I marvelled that this quality could so transcend all the pomp and ceremony, and the usual attributes of dignity.

On the second visit he realized that I was serious in my search for knowledge, and he spoke quite openly. In order to be quite sure, I questioned him again on the subject of our previous discussion. He repeated that he was always calm, and that this was achieved by meditation on God. He reiterated that he was free from all pain and free from all anxiety.

Then he disclosed a most remarkable thing. He does not sleep! He said that he spends the nights in meditation. Sometimes he would get up and walk about, but he never slept! In response to close questioning he said that he had not slept for years! It was impossible not to believe him. Everything about him communicated the idea of absolute truth and sincerity. Besides he had no motive to lie. Many of us may lie to impress our fellows; but this man had no desire to impress anyone. I had to believe him, and I still do, however impossible it may seem. He had practised yoga since he was eighteen years old. He said that he was really happy, and that this was achieved by meditation and renouncing all worldly things. In answer to my questions he said that he practised no postures or austerities. But to me it seemed that his whole way of life was one great austerity. Like other yogis, he said that meditation was at first a matter of great difficulty; but now it was no longer difficult. The subject of his meditation was always God. To other questions he told me that he had no friends, no relatives, no-one. He was alone.

The Shwe Dagon Pagoda

I had seen this great pagoda glistening in the sun as my plane came in to Rangoon. Burma is a land of pagodas. There is one on every hill-top and one in every village. They are solid structures in the shape of a giant bell; and are supposed to contain some holy relic such as a tooth or a hair of the Buddha. Building a pagoda brings merit, so that one will be born to a more favourable life in future reincarnations. This accounts for the great number of pagodas throughout the country; but of them all, the Shwe Dagon is the greatest. The origin of the strange bell shape of the pagodas is interesting. It is said to represent the most beautiful object known to man, a woman's breast. However, the shape of the pagodas has become stylized so that the majority of them have a long tapering spire. Most pagodas are painted white, but the great Shwe Dagon is entirely covered with gold-leaf. The pilgrim buys a little piece of gold-leaf, climbs up the steps, and sticks it on the pagoda as an act of merit. I was struck with wonder. At times I have travelled far to see some shrine or place of veneration only to find myself unmoved when I got there. I remember going to the Sistine Chapel. I had read so much about it, I wanted to experience it in full. But nothing happened. I was unmoved. No matter how much I tried to experience the atmosphere of this sacred place, all I could think of was the crowd of American tourists milling around me. But wonder came to me at the Shwe Dagon Pagoda. And awe. I stayed there a long time. Then I went to the little place where the priest sells the gold-leaf. Like the other pilgrims I bought my little square of gold. Then I climbed the steps and stuck it on the base of the great dome. It seemed such a tiny little piece, and all the immensity of the dome was there before me.

Pilgrims who lack the material necessities of life come to the pagoda. Many of them have nothing; yet they buy their little pieces of gold-leaf with what they have. What a waste! Would it not be better if they bought some rice for their children? And I watched them for a long time. And I came to understand that it is not wasted. They gain something very precious. You can see it in their faces. And I think I did too. And if ever I return to Rangoon I shall do the same again. But there is the rub. It could never be the same again. Things are never the same again however much we might wish it. And perhaps women know this better than men. If we would only stop to think, we would not expect it so often. The first time is a unique experience in anything we do, whether it be visiting the Shwe Dagon Pagoda or looking at the Mona Lisa. The second time is never the same as the first. It may be better, and it often is. Last time I was in Paris I went to the Louvre as I usually do but this time I was very fortunate. There was no-one else looking at the picture. I stood there a long time. Then suddenly I realized that I was smiling back!

The Buddhist religion has split into two great schools, Hinayana, or the Lesser Vehicle, and Mahayana, or the Greater Vehicle. The Shwe Dagon is a leading centre of Hinayana. This emphasizes austerity and personal example. It is the religion of Burma, Thailand, Cambodia, Laos and Ceylon. Mahayana is more concerned with faith and good works, and thus has a greater appeal to the common man. It extended north to China and thence to Tibet and Japan. Hinayana has its saffron robed monks that we see in the streets of Colombo and Bangkok. I remember once driving through Bangkok at dawn to catch an early plane. The streets were full of monks each with his begging bowl. All who passed put something in the bowl, but the monk looked neither to right nor left, and gave no thanks. He who giveth receiveth. A few days later I fell into conversation with the man sitting next to me on a long flight. He turned out to be an American who was responsible for doling out aid to one of the South East Asian countries. I shall not name the country for fear of identifying him. He was disgruntled in the extreme, and was ready to grizzle to anyone who would listen.

'We give them millions, and they hardly say thank you.'

I told him to get up in the early morning and walk in the streets at dawn. There he would see the monks and he would understand.

Giving and receiving. What problems arise from this simple process! It may be hard to give, and I am sure that it often is. But it is harder to receive, of this I have no doubt at all. I have seen too many patients tense and disturbed because they could not receive without anger. One might expect people to be pleased and thankful at being given something. But look around, and you will see how often it has the reverse effect. And it is not difficult to see why this should be so. Giving places the receiver in your debt. No wonder he is resentful. But there is more to it than that. As babies our mothers gave us their milk freely, and we were happy to receive it. When we were children, our parents gave and we received. This is a law of nature. It is set in our mind that grown-ups give and children receive. Then as adults we are given something. Unconsciously it makes us feel as children again. We are uncomfortable; we resent it; we don't like the one who makes us feel this way. This is so with both individuals and nations, unless they have that blessed quality which we call maturity. But then we do not give to the mature. It is the immature to whom we give. So there is no end to it, unless perhaps we follow the age-old customs of the Buddhists who give freely and expec no thanks, and the priests who receive without resentment.

2 INDIA

Research on Yoga

I flew on to India, and enquired at the All India Institute of Medical Research in New Delhi. In this I was very lucky. I was made welcome, and told that the Institute was in fact carrying out a research project on the physiology of the yoga state. But I was soon to learn that the project was beset with many problems, the major one being that it seemed almost impossible to persuade yogis to co-operate in medical research. This seems strange to us Westerners. The yogis are holy men, godly men. We think of healing, and the relief of pain and suffering as something which goes with godliness. But the godly yogi has little concern for such matters. The naïve Westerner might say, 'Oh well, we can pay him a fee.' We are accustomed to think that a large enough fee will enlist the co-operation of almost anyone on a matter which does not infringe the moral code. But this is a different world. The yogi has no possessions. Money has no meaning for him. He accepts only the most meagre offerings of food. Godly and saint-like as he may be, the matter of helping suffering humanity in medical research is no concern of his. This applies to the real yogi. But in yoga, as in any professional discipline, there are charlatans. These are men who are in yoga for what they can get out of it either by way of a living or notoriety. These people were prepared to co-operate, but not so the true yogis whose only concern is union with Brahma.

I soon became aware of another problem. The research project on yoga was financed from America. And to you and me it would seem a very important area for research. But India is an emergent country. Although still deep-rooted in their traditional culture, better educated Indians are seeking greater and greater western sophistication. And of course the Indian research worker is foremost in this respect. He wants to work with the most elaborate of scientific instruments and the latest in medical gadgetry. The idea of research in yoga, a traditional Indian practice which has already been studied for

three thousand years, does not appeal to him. I soon came to
see that this attitude of mind was a blight upon research in
this field.

However the researchers had been able to perform one very
interesting experiment. They showed me a glass, coffin-shaped
box which they had built, and from which they could take
samples of air for analysis. They had persuaded a yogi to get
into the glass coffin. The object was to investigate the common
claim made by yogis that they can be buried alive for long
periods without harm. The researchers thought that the buried
yogis might get some air from the porosity of the soil, whereas
in the hermetically sealed glass coffin there would be no chance
of any additional air. The yogi had stayed in the coffin, quite
calm and motionless, for some ten hours. During this time he
showed no discomfort despite the fact that the oxygen content
of the air he was breathing was very greatly reduced, and even
more remarkable the high percentage of carbon dioxide did not
cause distress or over-breathing. The yogi had merely pushed
the button which indicated to the experimenters that he wished
to be let out. When they examined him, he was perfectly
normal. The experiment showed that he had in fact reduced
the metabolism of his body far below the limits which were
thought possible. So here was some very definite proof for me
of the power of mind over body.

The researchers had been anxious to compare the electric-
ally recorded brain-waves of a yogi with those of a hypnotized
subject. Strange as it may seem in a country with such a
traditional interest in mysticism, they had been unable to find
anyone who was experienced in hypnosis who would experiment with them. I was pleased to do this. The subject was an
Indian doctor, one of the research workers. When I hypnotized
him we found that his brain-waves were different from those
when he was either asleep or fully awake, and in fact were
similar to those of yogis when they were in a state of medi-
ation. This was an important observation as I had long considered that there was a close relationship between hypnosis
and the state of mind in deep meditation. Later, the results of
his experiment came to fit in very well both with my clinical
experiences and my theoretical formulation about the yoga
tate.

The next experiment was to take this man's brain-waves
while I had him hypnotized and while he was subjected to an

experience which would normally be very painful. For the painful experience he was told to hold his hand in ice-filled water. This was chosen by the researchers as it is easy to measure the length of time the hand is kept in the iced water; and this is where my extreme foolishness could have led to disaster. Before I hypnotized him, he could only keep his hand in the iced water for a short time as the pain of it forced him to withdraw his hand. Perhaps I should mention at this stage that the subject was a doctor who rather prided himself on being scientific, and was more than a little sceptical of the power of hypnosis. However, when he was hypnotized he could leave his hand in the freezing water for a great length of time before he came to experience pain in it. Then I suddenly realized the danger of frost-bite, and possible injury to his hand. But luckily all was well, and he suffered no harm. While he was being subjected to this experience which would normally be so painful, his brain-waves continued as in the calm pattern of the meditating yogi. This, of course, fitted in exactly with my clinical work at home with the patients whose severe pain has been unrelieved by drugs, but who had been helped by hypnosis.

Traditional culture still persists in India even in sophisticated circles. A senior professor gave a small dinner party in my honour in his home. During it this fact was brought home to me very clearly. He was a highly trained man in his field and had studied in America. But in his home the inferior status of the women was very marked. Thinking that I was being polite, I made conversation with his wife, until I realized that all the men were talking together, and likewise the women were conversing only among themselves. The men hardly spoke to the women although one was herself a doctor. There were two attractive teen-aged daughters. Somehow I came to talking to my host about their social life and their future marriage. He made a great point of explaining to me how modern he was. Before their marriage the girls would be allowed to see the man to whom they were to be betrothed. Then he added, 'But of course they would never object.' And I thought of my own two daughters! Even in these days marriages are still a matter of arrangement after due consultation with the soothsayer!

Love in the Temples

It was June, and the heat in New Delhi just before the monsoon was really terrific. When I began to enquire about yogis, I was told that most of them had wandered off to the hills! For the ten days that I was there the coolest was 110 degrees, and each day the morning paper listed the numbers of those who had died of heat-stroke.

I am interested in Indian art, so in spite of the heat I thought I would visit the temples at Khajuraho. To get there I had to make a journey by train, and then hire a car for half a day's drive to the temples. On the Indian railways there are four classes, air-conditioned, first, second, and third. The train was crowded as if carrying refugees from the battle line. The best I could do was to push into a second class compartment. The heat was unbearable and the stench unbelievable. The man next to me was covered with oozing sores. The flies kept leaving his sores to try to settle on my face. The day wore on. There were wells at various stations where people could get a drink, but I was too frightened of dysentery. It was midnight when I left the train. It was so hot, people of the town were still wandering about the streets. Eventually I found a woman who could speak English. There was no hotel or place where I could stay the night, so I had to camp at the station. She sent for the only man in the town who had a hire-car. When I explained that I wished to go to Khajuraho, his face fell, but he said he would do it, and he agreed to pick me up in the morning a little before dawn. But when he arrived in his car, it was my face that fell. It was practically a vintage model, an old tourer with threadbare tyres and the canvas hood hanging in tatters. He had a friend with him, and with difficulty they explained that a bridge was down, and we would have to make a long detour. I bought a couple of bottles of soft drink and we set off. As the light of morning came, I saw about me the ravages of drought, heat, and famine. The road narrowed and forked, and narrowed still more. Soon it was just a bush track. At each fork we would stop. The driver would point one way and his friend the other. They asked half-starved peasants who only shook their heads. The heat made mirages on the track. We stopped at roadside wells and the two men would have a drink, and exchange a few words with the gaunt-eyed women as they filled their pots at the well. Then there was a well with no women around it. They stopped to have a drink, but there was no water. I gave them one of my bottles of soft drink, and had some of the other myself. Eventually we hit a road which led to Khajuraho.

With tea and something to eat I revived; and I set out for the temples which I had come so far to see. They are adorned with hundreds upon hundreds of luscious figures in every conceivable attitude of love-making and sexual congress. They are abandoned to sensuality. But above all they are beautiful in the extreme. Here beauty is in the act of creation and in all that leads up to it. We see the human body in all its glory, and those parts of it which are especially concerned with the creative act. From their expressions we know that they sense the beauty of it, and so do the gorgeous attendants who blithely help in these acts of love.

We often see aesthetic nakedness in art. But this is different. It is unashamed sensual nakedness. This is such abandoned eroticism and whole-hearted voluptuousness that it is rarely reproduced in detail in Western books of art.

It is not unnatural that these places have been looked upon as temples of love, of sheer hedonism, of all that is sensual and sexual in man and woman. But feelings of carnal sex come to the observer only if he seeks them. Otherwise he is transported by the sheer physical beauty of what he sees. And beyond this there is the sense of mystery. What does it all mean? So much love! So many acts leading to creation, and creation itself in so many ways! This is the message that comes through to us. The wonder of it all! The wonder of creation! The wonder of the creator himself!

Brahma, the creator; Shiva, the destroyer; Vishnu, the preserver; this is the Hindu trinity. In the inner shrine of every Hindu temple there is the lingam. This is the sacred symbol, the mystery. It is the symbol of creation. It is simply a rounded column set on a saucer-shaped base. Millions of people are drawn to it. They sense the mystery and the power. They make offerings and they pray in front of it. Perhaps many pray to it as if it were the God himself. They all leave just a little calmer, just a little more at ease than they were before. They are aware of the change in themselves, and feel that it is proof of the power of the lingam.

We, of course, sophisticated Westerners see in it the classical symbols of the male and female sexual organs. More, they are joined together. This is the ultimate symbol of creation. The guides see the symbolism; and so do the educated Hindus that one meets. But what of the great masses! The millions of half-starved illiterates who come in hope to the lingam! I doubt if the meaning of the symbolism ever occurs to them, but they are held in awe by the very symbolism itself. They come to it as something sacred, a thing of mystery and power. This is possible because the universal symbolism appeals directly to their unconscious mind without the individual's outward awareness.

Brahma is the creator, and the lingam is the symbol of creativity. Just a thousand years ago, during a great revival of Hinduism when these temples were built, the same idea of creativity came to find expression in another form. This is the creativity of man, his fundamental, biological creativity which in its beauty can resemble that of the gods. So the temples were adorned with these new symbols, man and woman in sexual congress in every conceivable way.

The driver and his friend were ready to take me back. They were all smiles. There was another bridge. It would mean a longer drive, but there would be none of the troubles we had had in the morning. So we set off. It was now mid-afternoon, the hottest time of the day. The road soon deteriorated. The heat poured down upon us. The torn hood of the old car flapped about, and the wind dried us up as it had everything else about the countryside. I did not know that next day I was to read in the paper of a startling number of deaths from heat-stroke in the province. The driver started stopping at wells to get a drink. At this stage I remember experiencing a strange feeling of superiority. Here was I, a European, coping with the heat better than the native Indians. But soon I felt it too. I noticed that I was not seeing things quite clearly. I opened a bottle of soft drink. It was hot and sickly in my mouth. I tried to preoccupy myself with things about me. The road was only an unmade track. I thought I saw a camel coming towards us. But it was a little up in the air. But it was a camel, because we stopped, and the driver spoke to the man on the camel. But he only shook his head. I knew enough to know that I was on the verge of heat-stroke. I opened another precious bottle of soft drink and splashed my face with it. And so it went on. Then at last there was the river. The two men in front turned to me excitedly and pointed. We drove on to the approach of the bridge before the driver realized that the centre was missing. The driver got out to talk to a man. I went to the bank of the river where an old man was watering some water buffalo. I thought of parasites. I thought of heat-stroke. I took off my clothes, and slipped into the hot, slimy water with the water-buffalo. My mind cleared, and in a little while I was fairly normal again.

There was a punt some sixty miles down the river, but the track was very rough. We had already had one puncture, and the tyres of the old car could give out at any time, but there was no alternative. I had booked on a plane from New Delhi the next day. There was still one bottle of soft drink. At dusk we came to a railway siding. There was an old man with a drum of hot water selling cups of tea. The tin pannikin burnt my lips, but I was now myself again. At the punt we had to take our turn in a queue of about a hundred ox carts. Then the train, and back to New Delhi. But the spiritual creativity of the erotic sculpture at the temples of Khajuraho was worth it all.

A 134 Year Old Yogi Saint

People in New Delhi seemed to think that I would have a better chance of contact with genuine yogis if I went up into the mountains. So I took a plane to Nepal. This in itself was quite an adventure in an old D.C.3 crammed full of crates and packages.

During our life-time we meet many people. Of all these people there are just a few who have some really significant effect on us. Sometimes it is a school-teacher or a wise man, sometimes a person of simple sincerity or even just a child. When this happens we are aware of it. It seems that somehow we have clicked, and the experience often has an abiding effect upon us. An incident such as this is known to the existentialists as an 'encounter'.

It was near Katmandu in the foot-hills of the Himalayas. I was still seeking yogis to find out if they could stop themselves feeling pain by some act of the mind. A guide told me that he had heard of an old man who lived not far away. So I was taken there knowing nothing at all about him. I had met other yogis, and at different times I have met many Christian churchmen. But this man was different. This man was completely different from any other man I have ever seen. He was serene. This was the thing which one immediately noticed on being brought into his presence. He was seated in a little clearing in the forest. It seemed that some invisible aura surrounded him. And when you were in his presence, the calm of it was all through you. Peace came, and body and mind were at ease. There was naturalness, and a feeling of unity with the things about.

At the first interview I knew nothing of the man, of his great age or his saintly reputation. Yet I was immediately aware of this aura of serenity. I cannot tell you what it was like because I know nothing with which I can compare it. He looked an old man. I would have thought him about 75 years. It was only later that I learned that he was in fact 134 years old, and that his age had been investigated by some of the staff from the Indian Embassy at Katmandu. But most important, and unlike most yogis, he could speak perfect English. He had apparently learned this about one hundred years previously when he had travelled widely on an extensive pilgrimage. He told me that he spent sixteen hours a day in meditation, and two hours asleep, and that I would be welcome to come and talk with him at any time during the remaining six hours. So I went to him each morning, and sat in the forest with him. And the depth of his serenity would fill me as we talked of life and death, of God and man.

First I asked him about pain, as this was the problem which was uppermost in my mind.

'Are you ever troubled by pain?'

'No.'

'Do you ever feel pain?'

'Yes. I feel pain.' Then, after a pause he added, 'But there is no hurt in it.'

These few words were to have quite a profound effect on my professional career and my life in general.

To feel pain, and for there to be no hurt in it! What vistas could this simple comment open up! For me, for my patients. For other doctors and their patients. There seemed no end to the possibilities. I felt the urgent need to listen and learn, so that I could take something back with me from this saint-like man of 134. As I sat there in the forest the importance of what he had said seemed enormous. And of course it is enormous.

With further questioning he explained things to me more clearly. If he trod on a tack, he would be aware that something was wrong and he would move his foot. But there was no pain, not even discomfort as we ordinarily know it. Surely this was the nervous system working at a level of adjustment which neared perfection. Yet in the strange atmosphere of this saintly man it seemed quite natural and just what one should expect.

These few words, incongruous in themselves, that pain need not hurt, did in fact start me off on a series of investigations with other mystics, and experiments, both on myself and on my patients. It was not long after I returned home before I found that I could relax my own mind to a state of consciousness somewhat similar to yoga meditation. I found that in this state of mind, stimuli which normally would be quite painful became matters of little consequence, and lost their hurt just as the old man had described to me.

Then the great chance came; and like so many important chances I nearly missed it. I had a decayed tooth that had to come out. It was obvious that I could use this to prove my theories. On the other hand, this would involve a far greater test of control than anything I had tried; and I was well aware if I were unable to maintain the necessary state of mind, I would be precipitated into severe pain. I thought about it a lot, and came to the conclusion that it was really important to put the old yogi's ideas to the test. My usual dentist does not do extractions and he referred me to a dental surgeon. But instead I consulted a dentist friend, and asked him if he would co-operate in an experiment, and take out my tooth without any anaesthetic. At first he was against the idea. However, he finally agreed to take an x-ray to see how difficult the job would be. The next day he 'phoned saying that the x-ray showed that it would be a difficult extraction and that he was not prepared to do it without an anaesthetic. I thought my experiment had fallen through, but by a stroke of luck a few days later I met him again quite accidentally in the street. I explained that the experiment was important to me, and that I would not hold it against him if I were hurt in the process. He then agreed to do it. I mention this background just to indicate that the experiment got away to a rather bad start which would have the psychological effect of making things more difficult. There is another point I should mention. I am in no way a tough he-man. Under normal circumstances I am particularly sensitive to pain. I arranged with the dentist that I would sit with my elbow on the arm of the dental chair with my hand in the air. When I let my hand fall down I would be ready for him to do what had to be done. On the appointed day I relaxed very completely for half an hour; then walked to the surgery, sat in the chair, relaxed again and in a few moments signalled with my hand that I was ready. He got to work and pulled out the tooth. As with the yogi, I felt the pain, but there was no hurt to it. This of course sounds strange to unfamiliar ears. It is hard to describe a sensation when there is nothing familiar for comparison. The parts were not numb. I was aware as to what was going on; yet there was no hurt in it. I was not asleep as I had to remain sufficiently alert to co-operate with the dentist, who knows nothing about hypnosis. The dentist later told me he had to cut the gum and peel it off the bone. Then he had to chisel away the bone to the level of the tip of the roots, and then pull the tooth out sideways. I remember feeling the crunch of the bone as he was chiselling it, and I thought how strange it was that there was no hurt to it. Then another feeling flashed through my mind. I thought for a moment he must have given me an injection without my knowing it. I remember for the moment I felt quite angry. Then I realized that my friend would not deceive me in such a way, and that in fact I was simply experiencing pain without the hurt of it in the way the yogi had told me. The dentist was very impressed, and reported our little experiment in the *Medical Journal of Australia*.

This was all a few years ago. Since then I have had a cyst dissected from my neck and two other teeth extracted under similar circumstances. But much more important, I have been able to use the experience gained in this way to show a number of people how to control pain from cancer and other diseases for which the usual pain-killing drugs had not been effective.

So when the old yogi told me that he felt pain, but there was no hurt in it, he did in fact set me on a course of endeavour which I hope to pursue still further. But I would not have you think that the yogi just told me what to do, and I went home and did it, and then showed my patients likewise. This was not so. It was not like that at all. He spoke in English, but he used another language. He talked of the Hindu Trinity, of Brahma, the creator; Vishnu, the preserver; and Shiva, the destroyer. He spoke of the principle of Karma by which the soul of man gains merit, and above all he spoke of reincarnation of the soul into other living things after our physical death. I did not understand this language. Then as he talked and the days went by, I began to understand just a little. But all the time, the seemingly impossible problem was before me. Wonderful as all this may be, how can it be brought to the consulting-room psychiatry of the West?

I asked him more about himself.

'You appear extremely calm and serene. Do you ever feel tense or anxious?'

'No. I never feel tense or anxious.'

A man who never feels tense or anxious! As a psychiatrist

I could hardly imagine such a situation. On the other hand, from the aura of serenity about him, this was just what I would have expected.

Tension and anxiety are the major problems of psychiatry. Could I bring home his secret, or even some clues that might help? So I asked him. But he spoke in this other language, and it was hard, so hard to understand. He spoke of non-attachment. We must be free. There can be no attachment to material possessions, to house or home, nor to mother or father, or brother or sister, nor even to things of beauty. No attachment to loved ones! All joy brings sadness. This he said, was the inescapable lot of mankind. I would look at him, and I would let my feelings go towards him so I might understand how he felt. He was not sad; I am sure of that. Nor was he joyous. He was serene. How deeply serene! And I thought that perhaps in this very serenity there may be great joy, great sadness and great understanding all inexorably interwoven. As he spoke it seemed that there was some other communication of meaning, something quite apart from any ideas which could be expressed in words. Something that can only be felt. And when it is felt you know it to be true.

I stayed at an inn at Katmandu; and each morning I drove to his place in the forest. After a few days I was struck by a peculiar realization. I was changing. I was less tense; I was more at ease. Matters which would normally have frustrated me were now of little concern. This was quite unexpected; I had not come for this. I was not seeking something for myself. I had come only to find out if pain could be controlled by yoga methods. Yet this change in myself was very noticeable. I was not serene like the yogi. Far from it. But without conscious effort on my part, I had taken on some of the inner calm of this strange man. This was more than six years ago and much of it has stayed with me.

I have thought a lot about this unsought and unexpected reduction of nervous tension in myself. It goes to confirm some radical ideas on psychiatry which I have held for some time. As you know, the accepted idea of modern psychiatry is that the patient gets well by being given better understanding of his worries, and by having repressed conflicts which have been disturbing him brought into consciousness. Now, the yogi knew nothing of my personal life. This was never discussed. All that I told him about myself was that I was an Australian doctor interested in the control of pain by the mind. And most of the things which we discussed are things which I simply do not believe. The Hindu Trinity, non-attachment, reincarnation. Yet this change occurred in me, and more remarkable, it has persisted. Furthermore, at the time of my talks with the yogi I was really under considerable stress. The weather just before the break of the monsoon was oppressive. Living conditions and the food were a constant trial. And I was trying to use all my available time in the difficult search which I had undertaken. Yet my level of anxiety was reduced. It is clear that resolution of personal problems had nothing to do with it. Nor did direct suggestion, as the yogi made no comments about my future well-being. Nor would it seem to be a matter of indirect suggestion as I certainly did not go to the yogi expecting some change in myself. Some authorities believe that the relationship between the doctor and the patient, the rapport, is the all-important factor in relieving nervous tension. But the yogi believed in and practised non-attachment. This of course precludes rapport as we usually think of it in the doctor-patient relationship.

Some years after my visit to the yogi I came to spend some time trying to find out what was the exact psychological mechanism which helped the nervous patient to get better. I had developed a technique in which I had deeply hypnotized patients painting, or modelling clay. I found that they painted things or made models which represented disturbing conflicts deep in their minds. Their conflicts were then discussed and the patients got better. Then I made the disturbing observation that many patients got better before their conflicts were fully discussed! So it was clear that some other psychological mechanism was operating as well as the unravelling of the conflicts. I concluded that this other factor was the particular kind of regression which occurs in hypnosis so that the mind goes back, as it were, and works at a simpler and more primitive level.

Now when I come to look back at my experience with the yogi, I see that a similar psychological mechanism was operating. The yogi himself was utterly calm. While I was with him I too would become extremely calm and relaxed. Sometimes there would be pauses in our conversation. We would both be relaxed and completely at ease. When very relaxed like this the mind goes into momentary reverie. For the moment our immediate surroundings are forgotten and our thoughts roam

freely. I believe that this state of mind is similar to the regressed state in hypnosis in which it functions in this simple
and more primitive fashion. In retrospect it now seems that
this is what happened to me in my talks with the yogi, and this
probably accounts for the lessening of my nervous tension.
Now that I am aware of the therapeutic importance of this
psychological mechanism I often allow myself to relax very
completely when I am talking with a patient. The patient unconsciously follows my relaxation just as I did with the yogi,
and he gains a similar reduction in the level of his anxiety, just
as I did.

The yogi spent the greater part of his life in meditation. I
tried to find out from him as much as I could about the purpose and nature of meditation. For the Eastern mystic it seems
that the ultimate purpose of meditation is to free one's self
from the chain of succeeding reincarnations. To Westerners
this seems a very strange motive; but we must not forget that
reincarnation is a very widely held belief. From discussions
with people on my various travels I believe that most Hindus
and Buddhists accept the doctrine of reincarnation as a fact.
There is a general fear of being born again to some lesser form
of life than we are at present. The Westerner must remember
that many millions of people feel like this, and many of them
have a particular fear of being born again as a pig. Meditation
aims to put an end to the cycle of rebirths. The mind is concentrated on Brahma. The process becomes more and more
intense until a state of supra-consciousness is attained. In it the
boundaries of being and non-being are loosened, and the yogi
finds his identity merging with that of Brahma. This leads to
nirvana and the breaking of the chain of re-births.

Descriptions such as this seemed to me to be but words,
and beyond my full understanding. One day when I had been
questioning him rather relentlessly about the nature of meditation he expressed the difficulty in these words.

'You can show a child a banana, but you cannot tell him
how it tastes.'

For a long time I had thought that there was a close relationship between the state of mind in meditation and auto-
hypnosis. I suggested this to the yogi, but he would have none
of it, and like most yogis he insisted that meditation was a
supra-normal state of consciousness.

There have been many theories as to the nature of hypnosis.

All of these past theories have explained some particular aspects of hypnosis, but none of them have explained all the phenomena of the hypnotic state. In 1957 I published a paper outlining a new theory as to the nature of hypnosis. This has become known as the Atavistic Theory of Hypnosis, and it has gained considerable acceptance among many workers in this field in America, Europe and the East. This theory offers a satisfactory explanation of the state of mind in both yoga meditation and auto-hypnosis. Very briefly the basic factor in hypnosis is considered to be a regression to a more primitive mode of mental functioning. Let me explain a little. In the process of evolution our mind has progressed to greater and greater complexity of function. In hypnosis it slips back, as it were, and works at a more primitive level. Our logical and critical abilities are lost or work in less degree; and we become very suggestible because suggestion itself is a primitive mechanism of the mind. When the mind has regressed a little in this way, it tends to lose its integration so that different elements of the mind may come to function independently in what we know as dissociation. It is this process which produces many of the obvious phenomena of hypnosis. In auto-hypnosis the individual learns to let his mind regress, and it comes to function in this more primitive way. This accounts for the absence of anxiety, and the feeling of calm and ease which we experience in auto-hypnosis. A very similar state of affairs occurs in deep meditation. There is a great feeling of calm; logical critical thinking is suspended, and the individual ceases to be aware of his immediate environment. At the International Congress of Psychiatrists at Montreal in 1962 I read a paper suggesting that the same type of regression occurred in yoga meditation as in hypnosis. This idea was strongly opposed by two Indian doctors. They kept insisting that yoga meditation involved a state of supra-consciousness, not regression. However, last year, 1966, I was in the island of Mauritius in the Southern Indian Ocean. Although the island is many hundreds of miles from India, it is inhabited mainly by Indians. I met there a very famous yogi, Swami Venkatesananda. I have his consent to quote him on this point. He believes that the state of mind in deep meditation is 'very simple' and 'undifferentiated'. I asked if by 'simple' he meant 'primitive'. He did not like the use of the word 'primitive' in this context as he felt that 'primitive' had a connotation of 'barbarous'. However it is clear that the ideas of this distinguished yogi fit in exactly with my Atavistic Theory of Hypnosis.

There is a further point of interest about meditation. Yogis traditionally meditate in the cross-legged squatting position technically known as the lotus posture. Europeans who write on these matters usually make some statement to the effect that this posture is comfortable for Asiatics. This would in fact appear to be so, as in all Indian cities one sees thousands of men sitting at the sides of the streets in this position. But when I came to observe meditating yogis very closely, it seemed that they were continuously pulling their feet more and more tightly under their buttocks. I questioned them about this and found it to be true. When meditating they keep their legs very tightly interlocked so that they are in fairly severe physical discomfort all the time. This seemed very strange. In the past I had tried to help tense patients by showing them relaxing exercises. But this had never been a great success. So when I returned from India I experimented in bringing my patients to relax in progressively more uncomfortable positions. The results have been dramatic. As with the meditating yogi, if we can bring ourselves to relax when we are slightly uncomfortable physically, we gain our relaxation through act of our mind, and not just from the effect of the physical comfort in our body. The therapeutic effect is quite different. If we lie relaxed comfortably in our bed there is little effect on our general level of tension; but if we lie really relaxed stretched out on the hard floor, the relaxation comes from our mind, and there is a lessening of our general state of tension.

Now we can understand something of yoga postures which seem so incomprehensible to the Westerner. Most yogis talk of subjecting the body to the discipline of the mind by the maintenance of strange postures. Different postures are often quoted as being good for different organs in a way that can have no scientific basis in physiology. But from what I have just said, we can see that the maintenance of an uncomfortable posture while in a relaxed or meditative state of mind does in fact work towards a lowering of the general level of anxiety.

In his meditation the old man contemplated the nature of Brahma, and from my discussions with him I gained some insight into the meaning of Hinduism. At no time did he make any attempt to influence me towards his own beliefs. In fact, he stated clearly that if I wished to meditate I should hold my mind on the being of Christ. As Christians we are so accustomed to the idea of converting others to our faith that we tend to assume that those of other religions feel the same way. This is not so. This is not a part of the yogi's way of looking at things. We Christians, and the Mohammedans, accept it as part of our faith that we should convert others. But any fiery evangelism is quite foreign to the Hindu and the Buddhist.

There is another essential point about yoga. The yogi is a holy man but, unlike the Hindu or Buddhist priest, he does not belong to any formalized religious body with a priestly hierarchy. He is an individual. He may stay in the precincts of a temple, but he is not really part of it. More often he lives the life of a recluse, spending his time in meditation and ascetic practices. Although there is a body of literature on the subject, for the most part the doctrine and the practice of yoga has been perpetuated by personal following, by the age-old practice of the pupil sitting at the feet of the master. And as I write, I realize that this is exactly what happened when I visited the yogi. I willingly accepted the role of pupil, and accorded him all the natural respect of master. This must have been one of the factors which brought him to accept me. It is usual for the real yogi to reject the European tourist, and even those in search of the spiritual teaching of yoga find it extremely hard to establish communication with these strange men. I learned afterwards that his acceptance of me was in fact real. Some three or four years later I was in America talking with a leading psychiatrist who was about to take a trip around the world.

'You have travelled a lot. Where would you advise me to go?'

I told him, 'If you want an experience that is unique, I would visit the Shiva-puri Baba of Katmandu,' and I explained to him how he could find the old man.

A few months later I received a letter. He had gone to Katmandu and had sought out the yogi; but when he got there the old man's followers simply refused to let the psychiatrist see him. He argued with them for half an hour. Then, just when he was giving up, the psychiatrist said, 'The Australian doctor told me to come.' Apparently everything was changed. 'Why didn't you say so before.' And he was im-

mediately taken to the old man. He too was struck by the
extraordinary serenity of the yogi, but I doubt if the American
psychiatrist profited much. I can imagine him with his cameras
and perhaps even a tape-recorder, and naturally the mystery
of it all would melt away.

And of course there is mystery. And I think I came to
understand more about mystery itself. We have to find
mystery; it is seldom thrust upon us. I am sure that many
people travel in the East in places where there is mystery all
about them. But they never see it. They have not looked. And
then the camera is the greatest weapon of all to drive mystery
away. To approach a holy-man with a camera declares your
attitude of mind just as clearly as does the loin cloth and
ashes of the yogi. But to find the mystery is not enough. Real
mystery embraces some hidden truth. In talking with the old
man I found the mystery of yoga belief. But what of the
hidden truth beneath?

I had read something of Hinduism, of Brahma the creator,
Vishnu the preserver and Shiva the destroyer, and the host of
lesser gods. So easy to think of it as the pagan rubbish of
simple minds. I had not even seen the mystery! God creating
and preserving were concepts familiar enough. But God the
destroyer! So different from our God of love! And very
different too from the just but punishing God of the old
testament. God the destroyer, who destroys saint and sinner
side by side! Of course, death and decay are just as much
a part of the divine order of things as are creation and preservation. The Hindu accepts this; and many millions of
Indians worship Shiva and the various aspects of Shiva as
manifestations of God the destroyer. While thinking of this, I
thought of all the patients when they are afflicted who say to
me, like they say to every doctor:

'Why should this happen to me?' He feels that God has
made some mistake that he is allowed to suffer in this way.

But not so the Hindu who accepts the process of destruction as but another manifestation of God.

When Durgha was Angry

The simple acceptance of the destructive forces of nature as
part of the divine law gives strength and understanding to the

Hindu. But simple truths become elaborated. A ritual is developed and another mystery is born. So it is with Durgha.

Durgha is Shiva in feminine form and terrible aspect. She is the Goddess of destruction and calamity.

There had been a fire in the city a few days before my arrival in Katmandu. The house occupied by two dancers from the Durgha Temple had been destroyed. It was clear that the goddess was angry. There was no knowing what she might do next. So at all costs her anger must be appeased. By coincidence the annual Durgha festival was to be held about a week later. There was real excitement, and the on-looker like myself could sense the feeling of urgency. The festival was to be held in an open space a few miles from the town. There are not many cars in Katmandu, but I managed to hire one. The road was clogged with pilgrims. There were men, women and children, and many of them had walked great distances so that they seemed near the point of exhaustion. All were bent on appeasing the anger of this terrible goddess. Many of them were lame and walked with sticks. Women trudged along with babies on their backs. Many were undernourished, some were clearly near starvation. Never had I seen such a collection of humanity! And so many of them with goitres, showing up as large nobbly lumps in the neck! And I remembered the phrase from my student's text-book, 'Goitre is endemic in the Himalayas.' And so it is.

At the festival itself there were thousands milling around in an open field. There was no chance to get near the central altar, but I am tall and the Nepalese are very short so I could see reasonably well. I was with a friend. During the whole day we saw only one other European, but the Nepalese were not concerned at our presence.

There were six brightly coloured canopies. Under each of these there was a dancer decked in full costume and with his face covered by a hideous Tibetan mask. This was horrible. But then, of course, the dancers were to appease the goddess whose being was horror. A priest threw vermilion powder over each of the dancers in turn. The crowd surged around them. The object was to touch the dancers with a finger and then touch their own forehead, and thus make a red mark on themselves with the vermilion. Then the dancers danced; slow, ungainly, and hideous in their masks. So it went on with people crowding about everywhere in what seemed utter confusion. Then I saw a procession of men holding aloft the heads of slaughtered oxen. I did not see the actual killing, but I was told that the dancers drink the hot blood of the sacrificial animals as part of the ritual. So Durgha was appeased. And I thought of my gentle yogi saint. He believed in God the destroyer as part of the divine order of things. But how different from the hideous orgy of the Durgha festival.

A Living Goddess!

Katmandu is a place of mystery, and it often comes upon one quite unexpectedly. My guide casually asked me if I would like to see the living goddess. Well, I have seen many statues and images around which some legend had grown. The sick have come there and have been healed, so the goddess must be alive. No, I was not interested. It was only when he asked me the same question on the third successive day that I began to take some notice.

'But it cannot be a living goddess.'

'Yes, she is a living goddess.'

'But how?'

'She is a girl, and she is a real goddess.'

Then he explained it all to me. There was a girl in the city who was accorded all the attributes of divinity. She lived in a temple not far away. Would I like to see her? Of course I would. So we went there. The place was filthy and my companions in the temple yard where I waited were a horde of mangey dogs. The guide returned and told me he had been informed that the goddess would not be seen today. So I went again the next morning, and the next, and the next until I was favoured by the child appearing on the balcony above me. She looked an unhappy little girl of eight or nine years. The sallowness of her pathetic little face was accentuated by the way her hair was firmly plastered down around it. Her mother stood behind her. Two or three priests standing beside me made a gesture of reverence. I did likewise. She remained immobile and expressionless, her big eyes staring in front of her. It may be that she was in a trance. In a few minutes she and her mother retired into the room behind.

I had seen a living goddess. My mind was full of strange

emotions, but perhaps the strongest was simple pity for the poor child with the expressionless face and the deep brown eyes. But what expression should one expect in a living deity? The Hindu gods have such varied expressions. Brahma is enigmatic, Durgha horrible, Kali as of death, but this girl has mystery in her face.

Her life, of course, is one long mystery. Secluded in the temple, she is denied the human companionship of children of her own age. One day each year she is taken through the streets in a huge wooden car, with great wooden wheels, drawn by the willing hands of those who worship her. In another part of the city I saw this enormous vehicle waiting there for the child's next outing. Then back to the temple for her for another twelve months.

But the mysteries of the living goddess act out in real life some of the turbulent forces which lie deep in the mind. This is the story which I obtained from my guide, and which I checked with others in the city. When the girl attains puberty the divine spirit leaves her. It is known that the spirit of divinity enters into some other child aged seven or eight of one particular tribe. It is then the duty of the priests to find out which child is inhabited by the divine spirit. This is done by trial by ordeal. This is an age-old method of distinguishing the good from the bad. The principle is that God saves the good and the evil ones suffer. But with little girls of seven and eight years old! And it is done in a particularly horrible way. Just as it used to be done in Europe, it is done by priests of the established church. The little girls are confined alone in complete darkness. Then they are deliberately frightened. This is done in the darkness by presenting them with terrifying objects in the form of the heads of animals which have been slaughtered in sacrifice. The children cry out in natural terror. But when they come to the child goddess with the divine spirit within her, she remains calm. This is the sign they have been seeking. She and her mother are taken off to the temple amid rejoicing. There she starts her lonely and unnatural life as a living god-head.

I asked, 'What happens to the girl at puberty, when she ceases to be a goddess?'

This seems to be the saddest part of all. She returns to the tribe and her family as an ordinary young girl. But of course she is not an ordinary girl. The mystery of it clings to her.

People are frightened of her. If she is not a goddess any more, what is she? She is a witch. They all feel it about her. No boy would go near her, let alone marry her. This is the terrible fate of the goddess whom they once dragged in triumph through the streets in that great wooden car.

Pornography in Holy Places

Nepal is a strange country. Perhaps some of the strangeness comes from its centuries of almost complete isolation from the rest of the world. It is only in the last few years that the road to India has been completed. Prior to that, one had to walk; and all goods from the outside world were carried over the pass by porters. No wonder it is a land of exotic customs and rituals! And the figures which adorn some of the temples are among the strangest of all.

I have mentioned the symbolic purity of the lingam, and the erotic beauty of the temple figures at Khajuraho, both of which express the idea of creativity. But many of the temples in Nepal are adorned with figures that are clearly pornographic. As at Khajuraho, men and women are shown in sexual congress. But they are not beautiful. In fact the artists who created them seem to have done all in their power to make them horrible. At Khajuraho there is ecstasy in their faces, but here they leer down at you to show that it is all lewd and depraved.

At Khajuraho the copulating figures are poetically balanced and integrated together in harmony. But here they are separate figures, each revelling in his own lust.

Every detail is shown, and the parts are painted in garish colours. Each group depicts some different perversion. Men are shown in sexual congress together, and I remember one group showing a woman satisfying three lovers simultaneously.

What is the meaning of such terrible things in a temple?

I asked a number of people about it and received different answers. Some said that these were warnings to the people of what not to do. But this explanation does not seem feasible. There is no idea of punishment for those who do these things, and in fact the figures frequently depict acts which would not come to the mind of most people.

Others told me that they were there to tempt the priests.

They put bad ideas to the minds of the priests, who would have to learn to be strong to resist them.

Some thought they were there just for ornamentation!

But the explanation for this pornography in the temples which occurs to me is different again. Brahma is the creator. We have seen how the idea of creativity is usually expressed in the symbolism of the lingam, but it may also be expressed in the symbolism of copulating human figures as at Khajuraho. It is common enough for symbols and rituals to lose their primary meaning with the passage of time. It would seem that this would be more likely to occur in a very isolated community such as in Nepal. Perhaps the temples were once decorated with copulating figures which expressed creativity. Over the centuries the purpose of the figures may have been forgotten. They then became debased, and we see them as they are today, something horrible and lewd, and seemingly quite out of place in the house of God.

Chinna Lama

The head lama in Tibet was the Dalai lama until the country was over-run by the communist Chinese. The head lama in Nepal is Chinna lama. The succession of the Dalai lama is a matter of priestly mystery. At the moment of death the divine spirit leaves his body and takes up its new abode in a baby who is born just at that moment. It is the duty of the priests to find this baby. But in Nepal things are different. Chinna lama is a hereditary office. This must save much confusion, but at the same time it probably lessens the power of the priesthood.

I went to visit Chinna lama in a state of great expectancy. I had already been to the old yogi and was enrapt by what I had seen. And I had read about the Dalai lama. What kind of mystery would this strange man unfold to me! Of course, if I had learned anything from the yogi I would not have expected too much. But at that stage I had hardly come to understand his teaching. He taught that pleasure brings sadness. I do not know what you think of this proposition; but it seems true that the anticipation of pleasure does in fact very often bring disillusionment. The more we look forward to some event the less likely it is that it will come up to our expectations. Our friends tell us that some play is very good. We go there in anticipation, and in our eyes it is not as good as we expected. Worse, someone we know wants to introduce us to a friend. We are told of his virtues; we look forward to meeting him; but when the time comes all we see in him is the ordinary run of humanity. The same principle holds in more important matters. A young woman yearns to have a baby, but cannot. Then when she finally bears a child the anticipated joy has somehow gone, and she is left with the feeling of being let down. So it was when I visited Chinna lama, the chief lama in a country where religion and ritual and mystery are such a part of every-day living. Of course there was an air of mystery in meeting such a man, but the strange aura which seemed to be about the saintly yogi was clearly absent. I soon perceived a practical worldliness about this holy-man. This was necessarily a part of his office, so why should I hold it against him? But I did. He could speak reasonably good English. He wanted to know what Europeans thought of the recent occupation of Tibet by the Chinese. He was worldly. And he had to be. He was head of an organized religious body in much the same way as is the Pope. Yet I felt that his interest in the practical affairs of life somehow detracted from his spiritual value as a person. Should this be so? Remember that I had just come from a man who had attained the quality of saintliness, and who had renounced all the material aspects of life. Are the two things compatible? Would it be possible to have both the serenity of godliness, and a concern for the material aspects of human life?

It seemed he wanted to discuss politics, whereas my mind was fired by my experience with the yogi to seek something transcendental.

'I have come to seek your help.'

'In what way can I help you?'

'Can you tell me something of meditation?'

'Like this.' He was already sitting cross-legged on the floor. He straightened himself a little, and immediately went into a deep trance.

The memory of this is vivid in my mind. In those days I was not as experienced in such situations as I am now. Here I was sitting uncomfortably on the floor, and my only companion, the chief lama of Nepal, in a deep trance beside me. I did not know what to do. I knew of nothing in the book of etiquette to guide me in such a situation. I looked furtively about. There was no-one in sight. There was no sound. I was aware of the thumping of my heart. Seconds seemed like hours. Then he opened his eyes, and resumed the conversation as if nothing had happened.

I visited him several times, and he grew to accept me in the capacity in which I had come. I remember one day he asked me how long I slept each night. I told him about eight hours. He was horrified. This was far too long. If I would only meditate for a couple of hours each day, I would need to sleep only half that time, and I would be better in myself. I have never got around to serious meditation, but I usually do some exercises in the morning, and after that I sit and relax my mind for a few minutes; and now I have rather less need of sleep than I did before. But then most of us sleep less as we grow older. As with most things, it is hard to find the real cause.

I had been getting on quite well with Chinna lama. Then one day he invited me to have some tea. I feared the worst, but felt I had to accept his offer as I did not wish to offend him. It was brought in by a woman whom I took to be one of his wives. My worst fears were confirmed. It was Tibetan tea, which is made by shaking tea with rancid yak butter. The smell was unbelievable. I gulped some of it down. As soon as I left him, my first impulse was to rush for my dysentery pills. However, I took a chance and nothing untoward happened.

On another day I was shown the residential quarters of the temple. These were occupied by refugee lama monks from Lhasa who had fled the communist invasion, and who were given asylum in Katmandu. They were recovering from recent privations of their long march; but they could by no means be called an outstanding group of men. I had thought of Tibetan priests as spiritual and unworldly, with a calm that could not be shaken. These men were quite young, and it may have been that they were not sufficiently advanced in their practices to attain these qualities; but they seemed as tense and anxious and as ill-at-ease as most other refugees.

They carried their prayer-wheels, as do most of the monks in Nepal. These consist of a small cylinder, two or three inches in diameter, supported by a pivot on a short handle. There is a small weight attached to the cylinder by a short chain. By gently twirling the prayer-wheel the cylinder is made to rotate on the pivot. Inside the cylinder there is a strip of parchment or hand-made paper with a prayer written on it in Tibetan characters. Twirling the prayer-wheel is the equivalent of saying the prayer. We laugh at the idea of mechanized religion in others; but there are many things that we ourselves do in mechanized fashion in the name of religious practice. Both the Catholic and the Muslim have their beads. And repetitive movement, especially if it is rhythmical, reduces anxiety by finding an outlet for muscle tension. Then there is the mystery of it, and the sure belief of the efficacy of what one is doing. Many of the monks whom I saw in and around Katmandu did in fact have a real calm about them. Perhaps the anxiety-stone is a secularized Western version of the prayer-wheel. This is polished stone of extreme smoothness. It is kept in one's pocket and during moments of anxiety it is rubbed rhythmically with the fingers, and nervous tension is reduced.

Apathy in the Mountains

There is a strange listlessness about the people of Katmandu. In fact the Nepalese as a whole would appear to be quite apathetic in most aspects of their life. There were few cars in Katmandu, and few roads outside of the city on which a car could travel. This was in 1960. Most of the transport in the country was done by porters along mountain tracks. The motor road to India had only just been completed. Prior to this, most of the petrol for the whole of Nepal was actually carried into Katmandu by human carriers. Each man would carry the terrible burden of four four-gallon tins of petrol. They are still seen carrying loads of incredible weight. The burden on the back is supported by a band over the front of the head. I was often worried that these men would get a fright when suddenly coming upon my car. But they never showed the slightest sign of any startled reaction. They seemed quite oblivious. They would make little or no attempt to move out of the way of the vehicle even with a sudden blast of the horn when the car was only a few feet behind them. Much to my embarrassment my driver frequently did this and completely ignored my urging him to treat the pedestrians with more respect. I had been talking every day with the serene old yogi. At first I thought that the common people in the street must have this same serenity, and it was this that made them so unresponsive to the motor horn. But I soon realized that this was not so. Their's was not serenity, but apathy. A terrible apathy hangs over these people. One day I went for a drive in a jeep along the new road as far as the top of the pass into India. Scores of times I waved to men at the side of the road, but never once was my greeting returned, nor was there the slightest sign of a smile. I thought they might be hostile to European tourists. But now I do not believe that this was so. It was this terrible apathy. I do not know the reason for it. There may be several. Chronic under-nourishment and over-work must have their effect. Perhaps there is a mild chronic hypothyroidism in the population. A great number of people have large nodular goitres that are quite noticeable as one drives past. It may be that many others have a disorder of the thyroid gland in less degree.

One day I visited a hospital. It was run by American medical missionaries. They looked sick. They were sallow and listless. In my heart I gave them unstinted admiration. Their way of practising medicine made me feel that my work in a large and prosperous city was insignificant. Then I met their wives and children. They were pale and wan and haggard, all of them. It seemed to be the old story again, that those who deliberately set out to do good often involve others who are less well able to make the sacrifice.

Where the Gods are Fierce

Buddha was born in Nepal. He was the son of a prince, and before his birth his mother had dreamed of an elephant, so it was known that something great was about to happen. He was brought up in great luxury, and care was taken that nothing unpleasant should ever come to his eyes. He was married to a beautiful girl. Then one day he left the palace and ventured into the world outside. He saw an old man. He was profoundly shocked as he had never before seen the effects of age. He saw sickness and poverty which he had not known existed. This revelation brought him to abandon his wife and child and his princely heritage. He set forth into the world. He journeyed from Nepal into India; and after years of meditation and privation, enlightenment came to him as he meditated under a Bodhi tree. Then in Benares he preached his first sermon, teaching a simple philosophy of life embodied in the Four Truths – Suffering is universal; the cause of suffering is craving; the cure is to eliminate craving – this is done by following the Eightfold Path, of right knowledge, right intention, right speech, right conduct, right occupation, right effort, right mindedness and right concentration.

This was some 2,500 years ago. It is well to remember that Buddha was a Hindu and that the simple code of ethics which he preached was in fact a protestant reaction against the orthodox Hinduism of his day. Over the centuries his teaching has brought a philosophical way of life to countless millions of people.

But in Nepal, the country of his birth, it has been different. We think of Buddha as gentle and compassionate. But here in the Himalayan mountains life is hard, and the elements of nature so relentless that the gods themselves are fierce. In these mountains, shut off from the rest of the world, Buddhism mingled with the native Hinduism and spirit worship to produce Tibetan Lamaism. Buddha, the gentle teacher, has become a god, and so have his various reincarnations along with the older Hindu gods; and in place of compassion there is ferocity which kills and devours.

We are all familiar with the classical images of Buddha. They are calm and inscrutable. As we look at them, we ourselves come to experience something of this calm. But the gods of Katmandu are fierce; we quail before them, and tremble at the awful image of things to come.

We can see changes in our friends that we cannot see in ourselves. Perhaps we can see changes in other religions which we cannot see in our own. The simple philosophy of Buddha is not unlike the teaching of Christ some five hundred years later. But the message of the Four Noble Truths and the Eightfold Path has largely been lost in the maze of priestly ritual of Tibetan Lamaism.

But there is mystery in lamaism, very great mystery; and of course mystery can appeal directly to unconscious elements of the mind without the step by step of logical thinking. It would seem that all the wonder of simple truth is lost; but it is not lost, it is merely replaced by a greater wonder.

The religious stories of Tibetan lamaism are depicted on scrolls which hang in the temples. These are called 'tunkas'.

I have one such scroll myself. Then, for the people, there are religious pictures painted on hand-made paper, which can be bought and hung in the home. I also have one of these. It is not a work of art. It is rather a garish green and blue pattern. But when you look at it, you can see two figures superimposed one upon the other. The larger figure can be seen as a man sitting cross-legged in the lotus posture facing us. The smaller figure squats with her back to us in a similar position sitting on his knees. Her face is turned so we can see the profile. There is a wonderful calm in both their faces which makes it clear that they are in the trance of deep meditation. This is a reincarnation of Buddha and Tara, his wife. These gods are in sexual union in a trance! How different from the simple teachings of Buddha! Yet it is beautiful, not only in the concept, but in the stylized form of presentation of my painting.

Beyond Pleasure

I would like to pass on to you all that I can of the old yogi's teaching. But you can see that I have not absorbed his teaching very well, or I would not express an idea like that. I said I would like to pass on to you all that I can of his teaching. This is desire on my part. But above all we must be free from desire. So it is clear that I talk to you as an eclectic, one who picks and chooses, rather than one who accepts a particular philosophy in its entirety.

'We must not like and we must not dislike.'

'But surely I should like the beauty of the forest around us.'

'No. That is happiness. Liking has a personal element which we must avoid.'

'But surely a man should like his wife.'

'Not if there is any personal element present. Love her, yes. But that is impersonal and brings happiness.'

'Should we not dislike evil?'

'Disliking it will not cure it.'

He then went on to explain that we must be beyond pleasure. Such an idea has never occurred to me. Although, when helping patients to control their pain in hypnosis, I had often put the idea to them of being beyond pain.

'You are so relaxed, so utterly relaxed, so calm that things cannot disturb you. Pain does not disturb you. You are beyond feeling pain.' But to be beyond feeling pleasure seemed something quite different; it seemed unnatural and something which I could not understand.

Then one day after I had returned home a woman came to me, or rather she was brought to me by her husband on account of her sexual difficulty. She was really a very beautiful woman, but she was tense and unhappy. Over the years she had seen a number of psychiatrists and had been given electric shock treatment without help. She was sensitive and at times looked sadly into the distance.

'I was Tom's girl-friend, but it was his brother whom I loved. This was sixteen years ago. I did not realize it until after we were married. It has been with me ever since.'

There seemed little that I could do about it.

Her husband was good and kind. But she said that she felt such a hypocrite in not loving him personally, that she simply could not tolerate intimacy. Without personal love she felt she would be debasing the act. It was her mention of personal love that made me think of the old yogi. As she looked into the distance I talked to her of impersonal love. Something that might transcend the confines of personal attachment. When I stopped speaking, for some time she remained silent. I wonder what she saw with her eyes so far away. Somehow she understood. Later she wrote thanking me for having done something to change her life. I felt I should have told her that I had only put into words some of the ideas of a very old and saintly man who lived far off in the Himalayas.

He frequently spoke of the three disciplines – physical, moral and spiritual. Physical discipline concerns the food we eat, the cleanliness of our body, the regulation of sleep and the control of our breathing. This latter is very important in all yoga practice. He spoke of a four-fold cycle of four or five seconds for each phase, breathing in, holding with lungs full, breathing out and holding with lungs empty. Such a cycle would give a very slow respiratory rate of three or four breaths a minute.

Physical discipline also concerns one's sex life. All yoga teaching warns against the bad effect from loss of seminal fluid. The old yogi advised that married couples should never have sex more than once a month, and when two children were born the couple should live as brother and sister. This was strange teaching for modern ears. As a psychiatrist I could but wonder at this compared with modern psychiatric teaching which puts so much emphasis on a full sex life as a criterion of normality. Whatever we may think, this man had reached a state of mind attained by no modern psychiatrist.

Moral discipline teaches the doctrine of non-attachment, and spiritual discipline concerns the attainment of supra-consciousness in meditation.

In talking of pain he said that pain was increased tenfold by anxiety and increased one hundred-fold by fear. We can be free from anxiety and fear, then the pain that is left is not too bad. This is the idea which I had worked on with many of my patients, as both anxiety and fear can be allayed by hypnosis.

I asked him about prayer. He said that prayer was very important. Prayer was like the preparation of a meal; meditation was the eating of it. Prayer expresses our love of God, in meditation we experience it.

Like most yogis he gave unsatisfactory answers to enquiries about supernatural powers. He claimed that he could communicate by telepathy. But there was no point in it. Therefore it should not be done. This was like other things which should not be done because they did not contribute directly to the attainment of nirvana.

One day he told me that in two years he was going to die. This was said in a casual and matter-of-fact way as if in two years he had decided to change his occupation. I subsequently learned that he did in fact die just two years after my visit.

I finally left him and returned home to Australia to try to evaluate what he had told me. This was the most difficult part of all. I had had the experience of being with a man who had so trained his body and mind as to be free of all anxiety and pain. Was there anything in all this that could be used, either directly or in modified form, to help my patients. I believed that there must be. But when I got home and tried to explain these things to my friends, they saw it all quite differently.

'Oh, what fun,' when I had thought of it, not as fun, but as something wonderful.

'Why on earth didn't you take a movie,' when I knew if I had tried to photograph it, the whole experience would have been denied to me.

'What a crazy old man.' Yes, but so wise.

There is nothing like your friends to bring you back to reality. I thought them insensitive, but now I realize that much of the fault was mine. There had been a failure of communication. I had failed to get the meaning of it across to them.

With my medical and psychiatric colleagues things were even more disappointing. I thought that I was on the brink of a new way of helping patients with anxiety and pain. But modern medicine knows that anxiety is relieved by taking tranquillizers or by bringing to consciousness the disturbing conflicts of the mind. And pain is relieved by giving the patient pain-killing drugs, and of course if that does not work you can always get a neurosurgeon to cut the nerves of the appropriate parts of the brain.

I became aware that my ideas were almost universally rejected. This hurt, because at most I was only suggesting that this other approach to anxiety and pain should be thoroughly investigated.

Rejection of one's ideas is bad enough, but it brings with it another train of thought. The majority of people whose ideas are not accepted are in fact wrong. I knew this. As a psychiatrist I also knew that persistence in the belief in some idea which is not acceptable to those in the same milieu is often an early sign of abnormal thinking. I knew that it was not uncommon for people with an odd slant on things to go to the East, and come back enthusiastic for oriental mysticism. I knew too that most of these people were a little odd before they started off, and usually returned a little more that way. These were disturbing thoughts. But I experimented little by little in leading my patients into a calmer and more relaxed state of mind with less use of tranquillizers and less exploration of past conflicts. The results have been good, far beyond what I ever expected. So this in itself is some justification of the old yogi's teaching.

I know that I learned a great deal from this saintly man. In fact, if he were still alive, I would seek him out again to thank him, and see if I could learn still more. This is my feeling towards him. On the other hand, I still retain a critical attitude. I do not accept everything he told me, nor would I want to emulate his way of life.

In a way the Eastern mystic is essentially selfish. He is only interested in attaining nirvana and breaking the ceaseless chain of rebirth. He has no concern for others. Within a mile of where the old yogi lived, there were people in destitution and near starvation. This was no concern of his. In fact, to improve their lot may be harmful to them by altering their karma. If circumstances are easy in this life, it may be more difficult at the next rebirth. This principle is widely held, and it is one of the main psychological barriers against the westernization and improvement in the standard of living in India.

Some principles of Yoga teaching are scientifically quite untenable. This appears to be particularly true of the Yoga teaching of anatomy and physiology.

Some of my medical colleagues, aware of these difficulties, especially the anatomical and physiological inaccuracies, reject everything to do with yoga as absurd. This is surely a wrong attitude.

I made this first trip with the object of finding out if Yoga had anything to offer in the control of anxiety and pain. The answer seemed clear. It has something to offer. But at this stage it seemed intangible, and I could see no clear way of incorporating it into modern consulting-room psychiatry. This of course has been my endeavour over the past few years.

4 BALI

Offerings for the Spirits

It is fun just looking at people, or at least I think it is. But you cannot do it in your home town because you are sure to be seen by someone who knows you, and he wants to know what on earth you are doing. In fact we do have to keep up with the Joneses, or at least appear to do what the Joneses do, and they don't do this. So I keep my fun for when I am travelling. In fact I have played my game in cities all around the world. A seat in a busy street is a good place. You just sit there having a rest. People walk past and take no notice. You can see their faces. The degree of tension is written there, so is their mood, their happiness or sadness. You can see if they are fussy people or slack from the way they are dressed, and the way they walk along the street. Some you see are wistful, some abstracted; sometimes it is all so transparent that you can make a good guess as to the thoughts in their mind. A busy hotel lounge is a good place, and you can learn so much about the person simply by watching closely how he talks to the waiter. Maybe he becomes more tense just at this moment, or his insecurity is reflected in his commanding tone. Airports are good places. There is a general increase in the level of anxiety. People are restless and fidgety here, and cigarettes are only half smoked. These things are not covered up by the deliberately relaxed manner of the pseudo-sophisticate. Theatres are good places when you look at the audience rather than the show. From the faces of people in Eastern bazaars you can learn a lot, but you first have to become one of them or your presence will distort things. Churches, mosques and temples are good, as people are usually off-guard; so is a club in St James Street where I sometimes stay and anxiety is relieved by an elaborate pattern of ritual. Parks on Sundays are good because you can see the way people react with children.

I played my little game in Bali. And I learned that people here are different. Of this I am quite sure.

I was going to America to contribute to a medical meeting

about hypnosis. My experiences in Katmandu were still very much in my mind. I had heard that fire-walking was performed in Bali, and I was also intrigued by a report that Balinese people often slip into a trance in their everyday life. So I broke my journey at Djakarta, and then took a plane to Bali.

Bali is a place of dreams. In the days of the Dutch, tourists were attracted there by the scenery and the simple charm of the people. Perhaps also the belief of Balinese that it was immodest to cover their breasts did something to encourage the Western tourist. But things have changed, and now it is only the older women in the villages who follow the old tradition.

Bali is a little island situated at the extreme Eastern end of the Indonesian group. Historically, Indonesia was settled by Hindu peoples from India. There is a magnificent monument of the culture which they developed. This is the great Barobudur in central Java. This was built in the eighth century. But the Hindu civilization was later swamped by further invasions from India, this time Moslem. As the Moslems pressed on from the West, the Hindus retreated to the East. Eventually the Moslems occupied the whole of Indonesia with the exception of Bali, the most easterly island, which has remained Hindu to the present day. This is the anachronism of Bali, a little Hindu island in an actively Moslem country. But there is more to it than this. The Balinese were cut off from the main stream of Hindu thought in India. In their isolation they came to develop a unique and characteristic form of Hinduism of their own. Two influences helped to keep their religion particularly alive and active. These were the continuous threat of the Moslems which persists to the present day, and the fact that the Hindus in their flight to the East brought with them both priests and princes from the other islands so that Bali became a real repository of Hindu culture. I have seen the way that religion lives in the great Catholic countries of Europe and South America. One can feel the presence of the Church. But nowhere have I seen religion as part of the everyday life of the people as it is in Bali. Above all it strikes the onlooker as a happy religion of a happy people. And so many of the rituals are celebrated with flowers!

The first morning I was there I noticed a little tray of flowers on the gate-post of my hotel. I pointed to it as I walked by with my guide.

'For the spirits,' he smiled.

As I walked down the street I saw little offerings of flowers outside most of the houses. Hibiscus flowers are placed in a little tray made by plaiting together strips of palm leaves. Sometimes under the flowers there is a small offering of food. The wind soon blows it all away. A dog comes and takes the offering. The little trays of previous offerings lie in the gutter. This is Bali. It is a different world. Later I was able to observe the mood in which the offerings are made. They are made happily and with a smile. The hands are clasped together for a moment in front of the chest. Then the offering is left for the spirits, for the wind and the stray dog. There is a blithe happiness about the way it is all done. It is nice to make a little offering to the spirits. There is joy in it. This is the magic which pervades the life of the Balinese. I went to the airways office. There was the same little offering on the counter. Later that day I was walking along the beach in the cool of the evening. A well-dressed young woman walked across the sand with that leisurely ease that showed she was in tune with all about her. She carried in front of her a tray with a little offering. She set it down at the water's edge, clasped her hands together for a moment, and walked back to her car at the roadside. As I watched, a gust of wind scattered the flowers. A stray dog came and nosed about and meandered off again.

As I walked back along the beach I thought of all the other offerings I had seen made. In the church the candle is so often lit in guilt and despair. In the temple they look to the incense, destitute, but with hope in their eyes. But here in Bali it is all so different; offerings are made with joy in the heart.

A Doctor-Prince

I played my game of watching the people go past. All that I had read was true. These people are calm, and at ease, and happy in a way that I have not seen anywhere else in the world.

By great good fortune I met a doctor who not only helped me in the practical matters of seeing things, but who also patiently explained to me some of the mysteries of Balinese culture. He was a native of Bali and had received his medical education in Holland. He was a scholarly man and when he knew I was a psychiatrist he was anxious to discuss various aspects of Freudian and Jungian philosophy. Somehow it all seemed out of place in these surroundings; and I noticed that I was not speaking with my usual conviction. Could it be that these principles do not explain the individual's behaviour as well in such a culture as they do in our own? Then when I had got to know him a little, I asked him the question which had been so much in my mind.

'How do you account for the calm and ease of the Balinese people?'

He explained that their religion had the effect of relieving nervous tension in a way that was hard to understand for those brought up in a Christian society. I had seen that religious observance was an integral part of their everyday living. It is just as natural to make a little offering in the morning as it is to have breakfast. As a psychiatrist I could understand how these rituals would work to reduce anxiety. But my friend explained some of the deeper significance of the religion itself.

The Christian aims to overcome wickedness. There is a constant fight between the powers of good and those of evil. This is a relentless struggle which has no end until evil is finally vanquished. The Balinese look at things quite differently. Evil is a facet of nature. It is with us. It is a part of the natural law. They do not struggle with evil and fight to destroy it. They learn to live with it. The two different approaches are reflected in the legends of the two cultures. St George is the personification of good, he fights the dragon, and kills this symbol of evil. In Bali there is a similar legend of the conflict between good and evil, but it has a different outcome. The story is enacted in a dance. Rangda, the evil witch, is not killed like the dragon, but is rather subdued and forced to the side, as it were, so as to allow a happy coexistence of good and evil.

There is another point. By and large, we Christians feel guilty. Somehow we feel bad that we have not done things well enough. We are inclined to worry about personal matters that are really of no consequence. This uncomfortable feeling lingers with us, and takes on the vague sensation of guilt. The church, aware of the widespread nature of our guilty feelings, explains the situation in terms of original sin. We ourselves perpetuate this attitude of mind in the way we bring up our children to behave well by making them feel guilty. Conscience becomes a punishing god within us. But with the Hindu things are different. The punishing powers are externalized as gods that can be approached in the temples with little offerings. The net result is that the Balinese is not plagued in the same way as we are with such a developed sense of guilt. He is freer and easier. There is less tension. Children are brought up much more permissively, and life is calm in a way that would seem to be unknown in Western communities.

As usual with doctors, our conversation reverted to medicine. There were only six or eight doctors for a population of about two million. Even so there was an emphasis on preventive medicine. Although my friend was a highly trained man, he said that he aimed only to teach two simple things. He aimed to bring the native midwives to wash their hands before attending an expectant mother, and secondly he aimed to have people dig wells rather than drink the surface water. These were the obvious priorities, yet how few of us have the capacity to put first things first. As he explained his simple objectives, I thought of all the Western medicos who go to under-developed countries with grandiose ideas, and quite forget these basic things.

During the days I spent with him I noticed how widely he was respected, and how promptly people did his bidding. One day I commented about this to my guide.

'But he is a prince.'

On further enquiry I discovered that he came from one of the royal families of the ancient Hindus who had been forced by the Moslem invasions to retreat eastward to Bali. Now he was using all the natural command of his royal birth to bring simple hygiene to his people.

His daughter was learning to dance in the classical style of the Balinese. In this, the dancers wear beautiful costumes and headdresses, and much of the dance is done with the fingers and hands. She had just been selected to perform on some important occasion. This was a great honour. He brought me with him to watch her rehearse. Although he said nothing I could feel how proud he was. As we sat there together watching her, I am sure the doctor-prince was thinking of the time far back, when girls of noble birth performed these very dances in the halls of his ancestors.

A Balinese Fire-Dancer

I wanted to see some of the temple dancing for which Bali
is famous. The dancers perform in a deep trance. This applies
both to the highly ritualistic classical dances done by the girls,
and to the dramatic sequences which represent the enact-
ment of some story from ancient folklore. I thought I might
learn something from these performances which might throw
further light on the nature of hypnosis, and so help me with
my patients. So I asked my guide. He was surprised that I
did not know what had happened. He thought everybody
must have heard about it. Every hundred years certain ceremonies have to be carried out at the big temple on the mountain side. The priests had recently discovered that these had
not been carried out as laid down by ancient law. Everyone
was terribly upset about it, particularly the priests. The result
was that there could be no temple dances until things had been
put right by certain purification ceremonies. These were elaborate rituals of mystical nature, and were to last for another
month. So there was no chance of my seeing these strange
dances with their entranced performers. I was disappointed;
but I was soon to learn that this state of affairs was typical of
Bali where religious observance of one form or another is the
continuous daily occupation of the people.

But I had better luck with the fire dancing. I was eager to
see this as it had a direct bearing on the control of pain, which
after all was the prime concern of my visit to these parts. My
guide drove me to a small village. It was dusk, and all the
villagers were sitting in the village square. In the centre there
was a fire of burning coconut husks. This was a rounded mass
about two feet six inches high and about eight feet in diameter,
glowing red hot in the failing light of evening. My guide
pointed out the man who was going to perform the dance.
He was standing a little apart from the others. I noticed him
go into the temple at the side of the square. I followed him
through the entrance gates. Like most of the temples in Bali
it was open to the sky. The dancer walked up to the priest. I
remained there watching. There were only the three of us in
the temple. It was all very quiet. The dancer placed a few
flowers on the altar, and then squatted in front of the priest
who mumbled a few words and sprinkled some water. It was

all very simple. Then they walked past me out through the gates and squatted down by the fire. The priest made passes with his hands in front of the dancer to hypnotize him. The dancer then stood up, and placed a kind of hobby horse made of palm leaves between his legs as he was to represent some mythical figure on a horse. He then sprang into the red hot mass of coconut husks. As he did so he kicked violently, and so scattered the fire. He now danced about kicking the burning coconut husks with his bare feet. In performing his dance he slid his feet along the ground so that the soles of his feet remained in contact with the earthen floor of the square. By this means it seemed that he largely avoided actually treading on the red hot coals; but at the same time he kept kicking them before him with the front of his feet and the lower part of his legs. The red hot coconut husks were soon scattered over quite a large area. It seemed that he was imitating a cantering horse and at the same time he kept kicking the red hot coals before him. This continued for some ten minutes. The whole atmosphere was eerie. I kept reminding myself that I must make accurate observations of what was happening. He finally flopped down by the priest who was squatting near the fire. I immediately ran up to him. He was in a deep trance. The priest woke him by sprinkling water on his face. I had brought with me a pocket torch, and I examined his feet and legs in detail. The hairs were burnt off his legs from his feet to above his knees. There was no sign of any blistering or damage to the skin.

With my guide acting as interpreter I asked him how often he had done the dance. This was his first time! He was just an ordinary villager. He had been chosen for the task by the council of village elders. The priest had given him protection by the simple ritual I had witnessed in the temple, and by the hypnotizing gestures just prior to his leap into the fire.

This was truly remarkable. Of course if I had examined his feet the next day, it is possible that I might have found blisters, as blistering takes a little time to develop. But my really careful and detailed examination immediately after the dance revealed no injury to the skin whatsoever. There is, another point. Dry coconut husks are very light. It would be quite easy to kick them along in front of the feet so that the red hot husk would only be in contact with the skin for a minimum of time. The action of sliding his feet quickly along the ground in the dance would protect the actual soles of his feet. But I have no explanation at all as to why he was not severely burned on his first leap into the red hot fire in which he kicked violently and scattered the coconut husks.

There are two matters here which require comment. Is there any explanation for the absence of physical injury and for the apparent absence of pain? As regards the first, all I can say is that I do not think that the sliding action of his feet and the lightness of the red-hot coconut husks are in themselves sufficient to save the dancer from physical injury. I hope at some future time that I may be able to make a full study of this extraordinary phenomenon.

The control of pain must have been very complete, and he must have known in his heart that it would be complete or he could never have been able to bring himself to plunge into the fire in the first place. Another point of technical interest as regards hypnosis is that the control of pain was maintained in spite of vigorous movement. It is usually easier to control severe pain by remaining passive in hypnosis. A further point is that in deep hypnosis the subject tends to lose touch with his immediate environment; but the dancer remained sufficiently in contact with reality to be able to kick the burning coconut husks about and to carry out the dancing movements in a co-ordinated fashion. Yet at the same time he was able to control the sensation of pain so completely.

To me this was a significant experience. It was an encounter with a different aspect of life which revealed the mind working in a way with which I was quite unfamiliar, and which I did not understand. The more I thought about it, the more incomprehensible it all seemed to be. I kept thinking of the yogi saint of Katmandu. He had gained control over pain, but he was a man of scholarship and high intelligence. He had achieved his ability to control pain after a hundred years of mental discipline and austere practices. In contrast the dancer was a simple villager who spent his life attending the paddy fields. Yet with the help of the priest he had achieved this extraordinary control of pain in a matter of a few minutes. There seemed to be an important lesson in this. It seemed to show that the mind had an innate capacity to control pain. It also showed that the capacity could be quite quickly and easily evoked if one but knew how to do it. I could not accept the idea that the secret lay in some particular mystique of the

Bali-Hindu religion. The more I thought about it, the more it seemed clear that this ability to control pain lay within the mind itself.

The dancer was in a deep trance when he withstood the pain which would have been unbearable in normal circumstances. I had already come to believe that the essential psychological factor in the trance is that the mind reverts to a simpler and more primitive mode of mental functioning. In spite of opposition to the idea, I also thought that this was an integral part of deep meditation as was the practice of the old yogi. This seemed to be a clue, that pain could be controlled by bringing the mind to function in a more primitive way.

Funeral Pyres

Of all the strange customs in Bali none arrests the attention of the visitor more than the custom of cremating the dead in funeral towers. The Moslems, of course, bury their dead; but the Hindus burn the dead body, and one sees burning ghats by rivers and temples all through India. But the Balinese, with their own special type of Hinduism, have developed a particularly elaborate ritual for cremation.

The body is burnt on a high tower especially constructed for the purpose. These towers are made of bamboo, and often reach a height of thirty or forty feet. As I drove around the island I saw dozens of them, either in the course of construction or just newly completed. My guide explained that the unusual number of towers was a part of the centennial purification ceremonies ordered by the priests at the great temple.

The body is placed in a coffin. But it is no ordinary coffin. It is made in the shape of a great bull, and is painted black and white. In every village of any size I saw men at work making these strange receptacles for the dead.

It is obvious that funeral rites like this are costly in both labour and materials. The Balinese people are not rich as they live on an overcrowded little island. So when death comes, a heavy burden falls on the relatives. Although this is shared to some extent by the local community, many families are simply unable to provide the bamboo for the tower or the materials for the elaborate bull-shaped coffin. The Bali-Hindu religion deals with these problems in a natural and realistic way. If the relatives cannot afford the proper funeral tower and coffin, the body may be buried until such time as the family can make arrangements for the requisite ritual cremation. The body is then disinterred and the remains burnt in the proper fashion. Alternatively the body may be buried and later dug up and burnt on the tower of some rich person, whose family is able to provide the proper facilities.

When these principles are followed the gods are pleased and all goes well. But the system is open to abuse. And it is here that trouble starts. It is very easy for the family to bury the body thinking that at some future time they will dig up the remains and accord them the proper sanctity of ritual cremation. But this is the temptation. It is very easy to forget all about old aunt so-and-so or the uncle whom they really did not know very well. The body is just left buried and no-one thinks any more of it. Of course the priests are all against this, that anyone should be denied his natural right of ritual cremation. The centennial purification ceremonies had to deal with this abuse; and it had been announced from the temple that all bodies were to be disinterred and given their proper rites by a certain date. This dead-line was in ten days' time. This is how it came about that I saw so many funeral pyres in the course of construction as I drove around the countryside.

This was the main pre-occupation of the people of Bali at the time of my visit. In fact in many villages it seemed that the whole work force was occupied in this nebulous project.

It was impossible for me to comprehend the full significance of all that was going on about me. What was the meaning of it all? How should I look upon it? Are they just a benighted people not yet emerged from pagan darkness? No. If we look upon it merely as a phase in an evolutionary process, we fail to see the underlying mystique. There is the question of values. We see here a very high value placed on the mystery of life and death, and a very low value on the mastery of the material comforts of life. And where has it got them? There is just about enough rice to go around. Children play unconcerned and uncorrected. They see their parents make their offerings: so they do likewise. They follow their elders into the temples. These are nice, happy places open to the sky and the air. They play in the temples, and as they play they sense the power of other things. And what is the result of all this to themselves? There is not too much to eat, but enough; not too much in the way of clothes, but it is warm climate. And there would seem to be some inner awareness that human dignity lies in the person and in his bearing rather than in his dress. Not too many can read and write. But they have this unmistakable calm and ease about them which seems so elusive to us in our land of plenty.

A Balinese Witch-Doctor

I do not share the view of so many of my colleagues that psychiatry is simply a technique. The patient says certain things; the psychiatrist says the right things back; and the patient comes to feel better. It would seem to be something like a game of chess. I believe that the real things of the mind are little touched by this mechanical approach. There is something very much deeper. But this deeper aspect of things is very elusive. It is only revealed on rare occasions, often when we least expect it. Sometimes I fancy I can catch glimpses of it shining through, as it were, in some of the people whom I have met in strange places. Can I put it a different way? You and I and any others who might read this book are so conditioned by the culture in which we live that these other functions of the mind remain concealed. But in foreign cultures we can sometimes gain awareness of these hidden aspects of our being. The different culture throws a new light on things, and dark places of the mind may be suddenly illuminated. These are important moments, precious moments. Then we think about what has been revealed to us in these unfamiliar circumstances, and we realize that it also applies to our own way of life. To me this is one of the great rewards of travel.

So I went to some trouble to find a Balinese witch-doctor. There was an air of the utmost squalor about the place where he worked. It was dirty, filthy. There were dogs everywhere, and excreta of the dogs lay in heaps about the yard. A woman was unconcernedly giving suckle to a boy who must have been at least four years old. The witch-doctor sat under a kind of open shed in the yard. He was a small, dirty man, wizened up as if all the good were dried out of him. The red stain of betelnut was all around. He chewed without stopping, and his open lips showed the mush in his mouth. He hardly paused as he spat in the direction of the large brass bowl at his side.

My guide explained to him that I came from a far-off country, and that I was a doctor like himself, and I had come to visit him. With the guide acting as interpreter we exchanged greetings. He agreed to continue to see his patients with me and the guide sitting beside him. He then carried on with his work as if I were not there, while the guide spoke to me, quietly translating what the doctor and the patients were saying.

Each patient came carrying a little tray of flowers. These were made from plaited strips of palm leaves just the same as those used for the offerings I had seen on gate-posts and in the temples. Under the flowers there was money. Sometimes I could see it showing through between the hibiscus blooms. Each patient set down his tray on a table which was already piled high with offerings. Once or twice I saw patients who were particularly well satisfied with the interview, add more money to their offering as they left.

His patients came with a wide variety of problems, aches and pains, infertility, difficult children, failure of the crop, lost relatives and differences with the in-laws. The witch-doctor approached each problem in the same way. Like a good psychiatrist he listened intently to the patient's story. Then like myself he used hypnosis. In my case it is the patient who goes into a trance, but with the witch-doctor it was the other way around; it was he who went into the trance. After hearing all that the patient had to say, he would sit up just a little straighter, his eyes would be half closed, and he was in fact in a deep trance. At these moments there was an eerie stillness as everyone knew that he was then in communication with the ancestors. As the patient waited to hear the verdict he would sit staring pop-eyed at the man in a trance in front of him. I have often seen patients watch me closely when I have been about to advise them on some matter of importance. But this was so much more intense. After all, my patients know very well that any advice that I give is subject to all the errors of human frailty. The wonder is that they listen at all. But with these people it is so different. Through the intermediary witch-doctor the spirits of their ancestors advise them directly and tell them truly and faithfully how to deal with the problem. This advice usually involved some simple rituals and the making of offerings at some particular shrine.

One of the most common problems was doubt in the patient's mind as to whether some distant relative had been accorded proper ritual cremation, or had in fact been forgotten and left buried in his temporary grave. Of course these problems had been all brought to a head by the centennial celebrations and the edict from the great temple. Some of these patients showed the external signs of chronic anxiety with which we are so familiar and which are so rarely seen in Bali. There is uncertainty in this situation, and uncertainty is a common cause of anxiety. But the great uncertainty of life and death, of whether or not one will be alive next week, does not produce the same effect because this anxiety is effectively stilled by the ritual of daily offerings at the altars of the temples. But for this particular uncertainty about the cremation of one's ancestors there does not seem to be any appropriate ritual. However it is clear that these doubts could be easily resolved by the witch-doctor speaking with the dead relatives in his trance.

I learned that, just sometimes, the witch-doctor's advice in these matters was subsequently proved to be wrong! Everyone has some bad relative or ancestor besides all the good ones. Just sometimes one of these bad ancestors gets in touch with the witch-doctor while he is in his trance, and gives him the wrong information. It is this interference on the part of evil spirits which leads to the witch-doctor's occasional errors. But he could not have made too many bad mistakes, as it was clear that he was widely respected, and many of his patients had walked great distances to attend him.

And so it is with us. I often hear of patients who do not respond to treatment, and of patients who do not accept their psychiatrist's interpretations, but rarely, how very rarely, does one hear of wrong treatment being given, or a wrong interpretation being made.

When I first saw the witch-doctor, I thought of him as if all the good had been dried out of his wizened body. I was too much influenced by his appearance and the squalid conditions in which he worked. He was not an evil man. In fact I believe that he did much good. There was nothing at all to suggest that he in any way exploited his patients. It is true that they were expected to bring a gift. But a little tray of hibiscus flowers costs nothing when the flowers bloom in profusion along the roadside. He treated his patients whether or not there was money under the flowers. His patients came to him tense and anxious, and they left him relaxed and at ease. I did not see any exception to this rule. No modern psychiatrist could hope for better immediate results. I have wondered whether witch-doctors' patients relapse more than mine. But I doubt it. I often give advice which is based on the cultural pattern in which I live. He does the same. And the thought came to me, how interesting it would be to investigate the relative relapse rate of patients treated by witch-doctors and orthodox psychiatrists!

Trance in Bali

While driving me back from the witch-doctor, my guide went out of his way to let me know that he was not over impressed by the witch-doctor's performance. It was the young man criticising the established order of things, for in this culture the witch-doctor is part of the establishment. He let me know that he too could go into a trance, and talk with his ancestors. He insisted that there was nothing very special about the old man at all. In fact many people in Bali go into trances and talk with the spirits of the dead. He could really do it just as well himself.

Later that day when we were at an unfrequented area on the beach, I brought up the subject again, and asked if he would show me how he spoke with the spirits. He sat down and quickly went into a trance. The stillness of the place was all about. On other occasions I have noticed how stillness intrudes on the consciousness when in the presence of someone in a deep trance. I heard the lap of the waves. A bird flew past. Then he opened his eyes and told me how Uncle So-and-so had asked how he was! He was quite natural about it, as if this were an ordinary, everyday matter. Now, if you or other readers did this, and people came to know of it, you would be in real danger of certification to a mental asylum. Yet the young man was not insane. Far from it. The experience emphasized to me how careful one must be to consider anyone's behaviour in relation to the accepted mores of the milieu in which he lives. I spoke to other people in Bali, and they all told me that at times they would go into a trance; and some of them, like my guide, said they could use this as a means to communicate with departed ancestors. They would do it when confronted with the problem of not knowing whether some course of action were right or not. From the way they spoke I thought that the ancestors became a kind of external conscience. You and I experience the dictates of conscience as something within us. It seemed to me that in the Balinese this process is often externalized, and it is the voice of the departed ancestors which says what is right and what is wrong.

The trance is a part of the Balinese way of life. I saw some formal ritual dancing in which the girl dancers were obviously in a trance. As the girls walk on to the stage their behaviour is quiet and demure as is considered appropriate, but there is some variation of expression, their eyes blink in the normal way, and they are responsive to their immediate environment. But as the music starts they become stary-eyed; they cease to blink, and their faces smooth out as if masks were drawn over them. In this state they go through the steps and movements of the dance. Then when the music stops they are still demure, but their faces regain their normal expression, the eyes blink again, and that quality of normal alertness which we take so much for granted returns to their being.

Before visiting Bali I had read that the villagers often go into a trance when walking between their paddy fields and their village. It was described how their gait changes into a pattern of completely rhythmical movement as the trance develops. I did what I could to study this phenomenon. I believe it to be true. The gait does develop a strange rhythmical quality, and the individual as he walks along appears to be quite out of touch with things about him, even to the extent of a complete disregard for an approaching car. When I returned home, I experimented along these lines. With a little practice I soon found that I too could walk in a trance. In fact it is not at all difficult. My walking movements become rhythmical and a sense of ease pervades my consciousness. There is a pleasant awareness of rhythm, and at the same time awareness of what is going on around me drifts into disregard. A feeling develops that the walking movement could continue indefinitely, tirelessly and endlessly. Thus it seems that the Balinese have come to use this other function of the mind in their everyday life. To them it is quite natural. They finish their day's work in the paddy fields, then they turn on the automatic pilot of their mind, as it were, and this takes them home without further conscious effort. By this means they conserve both mental and physical energy. It is interesting to note in this respect that long distance runners and swimmers use the same technique. They allow a rhythm to develop, and the body keeps on running or swimming of its own accord and with little conscious effort on their part.

I think the frequency with which the people of Bali go into trances has another important effect. This concerns their general absence of anxiety. All of us know that a good sleep reduces anxiety. In fact the doctor's first move in helping an anxious patient is to give him some sedative to take as he goes to bed so as to ensure a good night's sleep. The trance state has the same effect in reducing anxiety, only it acts very much more effectively than ordinary sleep. I have taught many patients who suffered from obvious anxiety how to go into a trance. They practise this form of self-hypnosis for ten minutes, two or three times a day, and their level of anxiety is greatly reduced. It would seem that the frequency with which the Balinese go into a trance has the same effect, and helps to account for the absence of anxiety which is such a conspicuous feature of their way of life. Incidentally, the same mechanism operates with Eastern mystics who spend much time in meditation. The meditative state is related to the common trance and auto-hypnosis, and so works in a similar way to reduce the individual's level of anxiety.

To Bring it Home with You

What we see in life depends very much on our own particular interests and our own idividual personality. Different travellers returning from the same tour talk of vastly different matters. Bali is a jewel of many facets, and some shine for one traveller and others for his companion. Some acclaim the girls; some the exotic rituals of the Bali-Hindu religion; some the natural beauty of the island itself. But for me the calm and ease of the people attracted my attention above all else.

To go to some strange place and observe things like this is one of my joys of travel. Then comes the challenge to study the strange phenomenon, and to try to decide what brings it about. In this case it seems to me that their natural use of trance, their rituals, their absence of guilt feelings, and the freedom with which the children are brought up, all contribute to their lack of tension and anxiety. But there can be more in travel than observing the peculiarities of people and determining what brings them about. One of the ultimate satisfactions of travel is to bring home with us something which we can use in our own life. I believe it to be true that there is something about the way of life in Bali which is good, and which they have to a much greater degree than we do. I am referring of course to their ease of mind and general lack of tension. Perhaps there is something about the way in which they live that we ourselves could follow to advantage without detracting from those aspects of Western life which we would desire to keep.

I have mentioned that hypnosis reduces our general level of anxiety, and so does self-induced auto-hypnosis. I have suggested that the casual way in which the Balinese go into trance helps to keep them free from anxiety. Now, we can do the same. I know this sounds a little odd; so let me explain. I am sorry to bring myself into this so much, but over the last few years, since I have become interested in these matters I find that I am very much less tense and my capacity to work has considerably increased; and this has happened at a time in my life when many men become more tense and their work capacity begins to fall off. So I assume that this change for the better in myself has resulted from some slight modifications I have made in my pattern of life. One of these concerns this matter of trance. First of all let us remember that trance is only a popular term for hypnosis; and that the essential factor is that the mind comes to work in a simpler and more primitive way. This is known technically as regression. It is shown most clearly by the way in which a person in a light trance is less aware of what is going on around him. He is less alert and less critical. He comes to accept things as they are without wondering why. From this it is clear that a person can be in a light trance, or even a moderately deep trance, without appearing in any way unusual to the casual observer. It is important to appreciate this. It means that many of us, perhaps most of us, do in fact go into light trances and think nothing of it. These are our moments of reverie when our thoughts wander aimlessly hither and thither. At these times we are regressed and our mind is no longer alert and critical. Then something calls us to the problem on hand; we are alert again, and our mind works in its normal logical fashion. Moments like this come to us frequently enough when we are on holiday. We lie on the beach and feel the sun on our backs while our thought go idly from subject to subject. We stand and look at the sun set. It is still and calm; we are thinking of nothing in par ticular; then perhaps we have moments without much though at all. After such experiences we are left with a feeling of calm and ease. In other words this perfectly normal and natura trance state, although it has only been momentary, has don something to reduce our general level of anxiety. We retur from our holiday less tense, and our work output is increase until our anxiety builds up again. The problem, as I see it, i that in our ordinary working life we keep our minds function ing at an alert, critical level all the time and allow ourselve little opportunity for these moments of light trance reverie. A lunch we have alert conversation with our professional friends at home we look at television or read the paper, both of whic keep our critical faculties in full play. Our ordinary patter of life is such that moments for reverie do not come easily. A a result we are denied these experiences of light trance whicl seem to be a natural psychological mechanism for maintainin peace and calm in active minds. On the other hand, my ow experience has been that it requires very little alteration t one's pattern of life to provide for this. By allowing the min a little time off, as it were, we not only feel better, but the fina output is much increased.

For instance, I have recently discovered that my friends o the average spend about one hour a day reading the news paper. In actual fact most of the news we read is repetitive, s only a small part of it is of any value to us. But most readin; of the paper is not done to seek information, but rather it i done in an attempt to let the mind unwind some of its tensio after the day's work. So it is with television. The point tha I wish to make is that instead of reading the papers and look ing at television to let ourselves relax, perhaps we shoul follow the example of the Balinese and let the mind relax i moments of natural repose. All I can say is that I have tried it and it works. And it reduces tension very much more effec tively than reading the paper or looking at television. Th reason of course is that these other ways of relaxing do no allow the mind these momentary regressions which appear t be important to our mental health. We are all well aware o our recurrent need for sleep. I believe that in another way w have a similar need of off-guard regression or reverie. I an sure if you all examine your own idle moments you will find that you yourself have these experiences in greater or less degree. If we develop the habit of letting ourselves relax in repose, rather than in these other ways which keep our mind active, these periods of trance-like regression come to us naturally just as they do to the Balinese.

Since visiting Bali and becoming interested in these matters I have noticed how continuously active are the minds of the people about me. There is not a moment wasted. I expect some people would comment on this with pride. But I doubt if it is anything to be proud about. Let me give you an example of what I mean. I usually lunch at a club. After lunch members gather in groups talking, or sit down and read a magazine. I do not think I have ever seen anyone just sit and be relaxed without the aid of some paper on his knees. In fact I think many people would be quite ill-at-ease if they were just to sit without this type of psychological cover-up, which allows relaxation of the body and diverts the mind from the problems of the day, but at the same time keeps it continuously active.

5 IRAN

Troubles with Officialdom

After finding so many things of interest on my trips to Katmandu and Bali, the next time I went to Europe to a medical
meeting I broke my journey at Tehran, hoping that I might
find matters of equal interest in Iran. But there is a lot of luck
in travel, especially if you have no introductions and just go
from place to place as I do, in the hope that matters of interest
will disclose themselves. The travel agents had told me that I
could get a visa for Iran at the airport. My plane arrived in
the early hours of the morning, and after endless delays by the
immigration officials I was finally told that this method of
issuing visas had been discontinued. I was then taken to a
small room and kept there by myself with an armed soldier
posted at the door. After some hours a higher official arrived
and I persuaded him to let me go to the British Embassy where
I would be able to obtain the necessary visa. I remember how
relieved I felt as I entered the building. Here at last I was
among friends. But this was not to be. Rarely have I experienced such real insolence and complete lack of consideration
as I did from the two young Englishmen at the embassy. I
suppose it was just another example of the government official,
the petty clerk in high places. But of course these young men
were not petty clerks. I only hope they no longer disgrace
the service from which you and I have every right to expect
help when things beyond our control go against us in a
foreign country.

A Happy Encounter

When I sought help it was not offered, and was in fact only
grudgingly given on my firm demand. Then a few days later
it was all so different. I was at Shiraz. It was a hot evening,
I had had my dinner and was sitting under a large tree in the
walled garden of the hotel. The place was quite crowded with

people sitting at tables, talking and drinking. At a table nearby there were three men and a woman in conversation. I observed that they were looking in my direction, but I took no notice of this, regarding it as natural, as I was the only European there. However the oldest of them, a man of about fifty, got up and came over to me.

Then in very precise English and with old world courtesy he addressed me.

'My friends and I have all travelled in foreign countries. At times we have been very lonely. We notice that you are seated by yourself. Would you care to join us?'

He led me to their table and we introduced ourselves. The young woman was a doctor, her husband was a bio-chemist, the other young man was also a doctor, and the older man was evidently a high official in the department of education. Then we talked. The three younger ones had just recently returned from three or four years' post-graduate study in America. They were young; they were enthusiastic; and more than that, they were idealistic in the extreme. They had seen so much, and learned so much, and now they had returned to their native Persia to use the precious knowledge they had gained. But all the difficulties in the world seemed to mount up against them. During their years abroad they had remembered the sick of their own land, and they itched to return to help them; but they had forgotten the ways of the Persians. They were frustrated on all sides. They unburdened themselves long into the night. I sat enthralled by it all, by their fire, by their idealism, by the force of their need to put things right. But I was not listening to them as a stranger. They had accepted me. I was one of them. And they showed the things that burned deep in their hearts to me, a stranger, but at the same time no stranger. And there are so many people whom I have known for years, who would call me friend, but who would never talk like this. The girl, her name was Paavi, black haired and fair skinned as the Persians are, burned most fiercely of all. Hospital appointments were made for other reasons than ability. The hospitals themselves openly had one form of treatment for the rich and another for the poor, if ever they were lucky enough to get into a hospital. Fire blazed in her eyes when she spoke of a politician's relative being appointed to some important medical post.

The intensity of a meeting of conspirators was about us. At

any moment one of them was going to swear to the death that he would put things right. I felt that some ritual was about to be evoked, something that would mingle the blood of those who felt this way and bind them together for ever. And such was the sincerity of their convictions, that I am sure I would have gladly been part of any pact they had made.

The crescendo of feeling of the three younger ones was rising higher and higher. The older man agreed with it all. He was possessed of the same fearless spirit, but with him it was more controlled, more directed and more productive of good. He now came more openly into the discussion, giving strength and guidance to the turbulent ferocity of his younger friends. The discussion swung from medicine to medical education to education in general. With this he began to disclose more of himself. His role in life was to bring education to the tribes. In Persia today there are still many hundreds of thousands of nomadic tribesmen. They move from valley to valley grazing their flocks and herds as they go. For the most part they can neither read nor write; but they are proud, and will contend to death their rights to graze their stock. In times of plenty all goes well, but in lean seasons when the rains have been patchy, one tribe may crowd in on an area occupied by others. Then trouble begins. My friend was a big man, strong and tough. He goes out into the wild country never quite sure of what kind of welcome he is going to get.

'I aim to get them before they have seen a Coca-Cola bottle.'

He was inspired with his work. He wanted to bring civilization to people whose nomadic way of life was completely unchanged since biblical times, who have had no contact with Europeans and little or none with civilized Persians.

'I want to bring them the things of our civilization that are good, before they are shown all the rubbish and trash by the traders!'

This was a real man doing a real man's job. At the same time it all sounded like the stories from *Chums* which I used to read in my boyhood. I asked him more.

'Oh yes, they are all armed, and are quite on for a fight.'

'Yes, I carry arms, but it is only in case of brigands.'

I asked him about food, especially about yoghurt, the bever- age made by fermenting goat's milk. The germs which produce the fermentation make the milk very acid. This acidity is such that it kills the germs which usually cause dysentery. He explained, quite seriously, that if you scrape the mass of flies from the surface of the yoghurt, and take it from underneath you are quite safe from dysentery.

He was not a man doing a job; nor do I think that he was working from a religious motive. He was just filled with the desire to bring something new and wonderful to people who had no comprehension of this thing he was offering them. And he knew that he must give them this in a way which would not destroy what is good in their own tribal culture.

Civilization is usually brought to primitive peoples by the the exploiter, or the missionary. But this was a new approach.

He fixed me with his eyes, and said, 'What should I bring them? What are the basic things of civilization? What are the things that are good?'

I have never been posed such questions, and the man who was asking them had to have some kind of an answer in his own mind, as in a few days he was off on another expedition.

'What is good in civilization?' I could not properly answer the question. Thoughts teemed through my mind. To read and write seemed good. But a nomad cannot carry books. To teach them to stay in one valley and grow a crop. But they have been wanderers for centuries. Teach them the rules of health. But they have learned how to live with the flies and the dirt of nomadic life. Teach them religion. But Christianity or Islam? This man in front of me, whose sense of mission so exceeded anything that I might hope to have, was a Moslem. This was perhaps the most basic question that a civilized man could be asked, and I was lost.

He sensed my bewilderment and at the same time my eagerness and my respect for him. 'Would you like to come with me? You could see what I am trying to do.'

This was an offer of open friendship if ever there was one. And it was from a most remarkable man, who had only just met me. I would have loved to have gone with him, and taken my chance with the yoghurt and the flies; but there was my medical meeting. I thought of all the stereotyped platitudes that one hears at an international meeting and the fearless inspiration of this man before me. It says little for me that I turned down his offer. I regret it. I missed a very rare opportunity to gain insights into human behaviour. But I suppose none of us is a really free agent. We all have our commitments,

and perhaps it would have been a little unusual to have disappeared for a month or two in the wilds of Persia.

The next day Paavi and her husband took me to their home
for lunch, and then showed me over the hospital where they
worked. I had not realized that Persia was one of the few
countries where opium addiction is still a major problem. I
was told that perhaps a quarter of the whole population takes
opium. There were certainly plenty of addicts in the hospital.
But I gather that it is only exceptional cases that require hos-
pitalization on account of their addiction. It is rather a matter
of the addict being admitted to hospital for some other condition. The opium produces mild chronic ill-health and a
gradual falling off of the individual's work. But in this country
many are born to ill-health from chronic malnutrition, and few
have regular work, and a little opium helps the individual to
tolerate his mental and physical plight with less discomfort. As
we drove back to my hotel through a slum area, and as I saw
the utter destitution of the people sitting outside their hovels,
it seemed that I saw things in different perspective. After all
I know many people who are addicts – to alcohol, to tobacco,
to sleeping pills, to TV – but they all have the material comforts for life and the opportunity for spiritual guidance if they
wish it; but these others are destitute, materially and spiritually.

Since then I have thought a lot of my encounter with the
four strangers on the hot night in the walled garden at Shiraz.
I have wondered whether the young doctors were able to
satisfy their desire to build a better world for the sick and
ailing around them. Did the educationalist decide what are
the basic things of civilization, and was he able to bring them
to the nomadic peoples of his country? There are things that I
shall probably never know. But memory lingers on, and I
remain enriched by the experience.

Persepolis, Home of Xerxes

The hot dry land between Shiraz and Persepolis reminded me
of the arid parts of my own country. There were sheep there
too, but I doubt if the Australian graziers would call them
such. They were in little flocks of ten or twenty, all shapes and
sizes, with long raggy wool, as many black and brown as
white. Each flock was shepherded by smiling youngsters clad

in bright clothes. A little way off there would be the tents in which they lived. These were all black, and this seemed to make them look hotter than ever in the blazing sun. In other places there were families on the move. Sheep, goats, asses and camels plodding along together. Then followed the beasts of burden, other asses and camels piled high with tents and cooking gear with the old men and women of the tribe perched precariously on top. These were the more adventurous of the nomads, those who would come to the edge of civilization, as it were, but still would have nothing of it.

I arrived at Persepolis in the midday heat. Many of us have visited Athens and have seen the Parthenon and the other ancient monuments; and I expect most of us at one time or another have read about the culture which produced these enduring relics. I have; and perhaps like me you have fallen into the way of thinking of the highly civilized ancient Greeks fighting the almost barbarous Persians. One glance at Persepolis will show how wrong this is. These remains point to a civilization of great grandeur. In fact, as I wandered among the great columns, thoughts of Athens kept coming to my mind. There is such similarity, and at the same time such difference.

The ruins look out over an open plain, boundless and bare. Behind, there are steep barren hills. There is a small restaurant nearby – that is all. It was too hot for my guide. He showed no desire to accompany me around the ruins, and left me at the gate. It was better this way. The ghosts of the past will come and disclose themselves to you when you are alone. You do not see them. But you feel their presence, and know that they are there. But with a guide they stay away and you have lost it all. He will give you the facts and the figures, but this drives away the magic. This was the place built by Darius, and on these very stones strode the great Xerxes. I stood in the scant shade of one of the great columns. Some of them are still surmounted by their strange capitals in the form of double-headed bulls. There was not a living soul about. From this place Xerxes had controlled most of the known world. It was eerie, or was it just the heat playing tricks with my mind. I sat on a stone from one of the broken columns and thought about it. A lizard came and sat next to me. There were just the two of us. Then I went on to the remains of the giant stairway. There was a notice on the side of it for all to read. Beside it there was posted up an English translation. I read it. I was moved by the simple poetry of what I read. So I read it again. And I thought to myself I shall remember these words. This is what I remember.

'There is a great god Ahura-Mazda, the creator of the skies, of the earth, of men and fellowship among men, who made Xerxes king. I am Xerxes, king of all the lands, king of all the tribes, king of all men.'

I read the notice just as Xerxes' men had read it. And like them I wondered at the man who could lead his warriors from here in Southern Persia to the very outskirts of Athens.

Then I thought of Shelley's poem.

'My name is Ozymandias, king of kings:
Look on my works, ye Mighty, and despair!
Nothing beside remains. Round the decay
Of that colossal wreck, boundless and bare,
The lone and level sands stretch far away.'

No, something does remain. I felt inspired by it. The inspiration of it all remains, the greatness and the resolve. And if you can let yourself imagine these things, I am sure that you too can share in it.

I drove on in the heat and the stillness to the place where Cyrus is buried in a little tomb on the open plain. This is where he defeated the Medes in the sixth century B.C. There was an English translation of the simple inscription.

'I am Cyrus who founded the Empire of the Persians.
Begrudge me not this plot of earth that covers my body.'

Ahura-Mazda

The ancient Persians, or Achaemenids, as they are called, after Achaemenes the founder of the dynasty, worshipped Ahura Mazda. This was God personified in the spirit of light. I wonder how many people who use the popular Mazda electric light bulbs know the origin of the name.

This is a religion of great antiquity. I climbed a high hill to see the remains of one of the temples. But two or three thousand years had left only a few stones. It was probably in the seventh century B.C. that the prophet Zoroaster reformed the religion. Ahura-Mazda, representing the powers of good ness and light, is always threatened by the powers of darkness and evil. The prophet codified his teaching in his writings, the Zend-avesta, and this became the bible of the Zoroastrians. But much of the Zend-avesta was destroyed when Persepolis was burned by Alexander the Great in 330 B.C. He had conquered the Persians, and during an orgy in the palace set fire to it, it is said at the instigation of his mistress Thais. But Zoroastrianism persisted as the religion of the Persians until the Arab invasion and the substitution of Islam in the seventh century A.D.

At the present time the religion of Xerxes and those who built Persepolis survives with the Parsees of India. These people of Persian origin live mainly around Bombay. In that city are the Towers of Silence. This is where the Parsees expose their dead to be devoured by vultures. As you drive past you can see dozens of these horrible birds perched in nearby trees awaiting the next human offering. Sometimes they can be seen flying away from the towers with bits of human flesh in their beaks.

When life is finished, it seems that man is uncertain how to dispose of his dead body. The Hindus burn their dead, while the Moslems bury theirs. The present day Protestant has a choice, while the Catholic prefers burial. The ancient Egyptians tried to preserve the body by mummification. But the Parsees, guardians of the Zoroastrian faith of Xerxes, in offering the body to the vultures have the strangest way of all.

In the Great Square at Isfahan

It was late afternoon, and I was sitting in the great square of Isfahan quietly absorbing the life that was going on around me. On one side was the Blue Mosque, majestic and inspiring; and at the other was the covered bazaar with its teeming thousands scrambling for the stuff of life. Then I noticed near at hand a group of students. They were eyeing me, and obviously talking about me. This was natural enough as there were few Europeans about. They were happy. Each was nudging his neighbour as if daring him to do something. It seemed that they were about to play some trick on me. But they seemed in good humour, so rather than retreat to my hotel, I just sat there and waited. Eventually two of them approached me, while the others remained a little way off watching.

'Hello.'

'Hello.'

Then in faltering English, 'Are you an American?'

'No.'

'Are you English?'

'No, I am Australian.'

I now realized what it was all about. They wanted to try out the English which they had learned at school. The conversation proceeded.

'Is Australia near England?'

'No.'

'Is it near France?'

'No. It is a long way from England and France.'

There was quite a pause. I was not helping too much. Then 'Can you read English?'

'Yes.' At this moment they both thrust their school exercise books in front of me. Suddenly the ice was broken. They all crowded around me, ten or a dozen of them thrusting forward their books. Of all things, it was a passage from Hamlet. I did their homework for them, and they left in high glee. I thought no more of it until the next evening. I was again in the great square. The news had got about. They were all waiting for me. Not ten or a dozen but twenty or thirty. There was something infectious about their eagerness and good humour. One would ask me something, then another would put some question which he had obviously been saying over and over to himself. And so it went on. Never have I had such a crazy conversation. And there was fun in it, both for them and for me. When at last I tired, they would hardly let me go.

But why Hamlet? Shakespeare for you and me, yes. But surely not for the students of Isfahan. But this is not unique. I remember once talking with a Japanese doctor in Kyoto. He seemed to be speaking well, but at the same time quite strangely. Then I realized that his English was based on his reading of Shakespeare.

I was thinking about this. Shakespearean English, of course is inappropriate to ordinary conversation. One of the most important things in psychiatry is the correct assessment of minor degrees of inappropriate behaviour. It may be of no significance at all as with the foreign students of Shakespeare, or it may be an early sight of schizophrenic illness. It is frequently seen as a slight inappropriateness of dress. A girl who would normally wear a dress suitable to the occasion may take to wearing clothes that are correct in themselves, but at the same time are not quite suitable to the occasion on which she wears them. Or it may be something quite simple. Costume jewellery may be worn which is quite fashionable in itself, but at the same time is not in keeping with the particular dress. The mind is somehow losing its sense of natural harmony. A man may dress too formally or too informally for the particular occasion, or may smoke in circumstances in which he would not ordinarily smoke. These are very simple things, but they disclose a slightly inappropriate reaction on the part of the individual. You may say that all this is too subtle, that anyone can make mistakes. Quite so, but the fact remains that I have seen many people, particularly young people, who have shown slightly inappropriate reactions like these, and then a few months later have displayed clear signs of a schizophrenic behaviour. Sometimes the inappropriateness is due to inattention to detail, but such inattention itself is significant particularly if it is something new. On the other hand, this type of inappropriate response cannot be easily avoided by taking care. It often happens that the more the individual thinks about the matter, the more inappropriate the response becomes. When we come to think about it, the ability to make the suitable response is something which comes naturally and intuitively. As soon as we begin to scrutinize the situation we lose our spontaneity. Is it appropriate to wander so far from the great square at Isfahan? But is it Isfahan that I really want to talk about, or is it these other things, the strange shadows which we can only see when the substance is far away?

In the Blue Mosque

I sat in the Blue Mosque of Isfahan. All told I must have sat there for many hours. If you are relaxed, and can let it be known by what you do that you are at ease, then the passer-by is unconcerned and does not bother you. And this applies to more situations than just sitting in a mosque. Men came. They washed their hands, their faces and their feet at the font in the forecourt. They faced towards Mecca. They knelt, and prayed and repeated verses from the Koran. In contrast to our own church there were many times more men than women. And the women who did come were segregated behind a screen. At different times I have asked guides and others about the predominence of men in the mosques, but I have never received a really satisfactory explanation. The usual answer has been, 'Oh, they can pray and read the Koran at home.' As I see it, there is probably a number of psychological reasons. Although the word 'Islam' means 'Surrender' in the sense of surrender to Allah, it is essentially a virile religion. It is a man's faith. In this respect it contrasts sharply with Christianity with its emphasis on love and passivity which are essential traits of the mature female personality. Then there are social influences. Islam has had its origin and growth in lands which have held women in subservience for centuries, while Christianity has spread in countries which were socially ready for the further emancipation of women. These same principles apply in the present day when Islam rather than Christianity is spreading in the African countries where Negro women still have a vastly inferior status to men. Here in Persia, emancipation is proceeding rapidly. The veil is dropping out of use. But the Moslem can still have four wives, and in fact women do not share equally with men in the worship of God in the mosques.

I often experience a deep sense of the spiritual in a mosque which I feel is so often lacking in our own churches. The atmosphere of the mosque is different, and the spiritual feeling of the holy place is enhanced by the absence of life-like images.

Our Catholic churches are filled with images of Madonna and Child. We see the Son of God depicted on the cross; and in the Sistine Chapel Michelangelo painted God himself. But in no mosque is there any image of Allah or Mahommed, his prophet. In place of this the ornamentation takes the form of verses from the Koran reproduced in highly stylized lettering so that beautiful patterns result. In the great mosques this is usually done in black marble in-lay on a background of white.

Sometimes repetition of patterns of stylized flowers are used as added decoration. Of these the tulip is a common theme.

While wandering around mosques I have often noticed places where the tulip pattern is so stylized as to become classical Freudian symbol of sex. It would seem that this sym bol must unconsciously appeal to people. We think it nice; we think it interesting; but the censoring mechanism of the mind ordinarily denies us understanding as to why we find the pattern so attractive.

I have done some work in helping mentally ill patients by bringing them to express themselves in painting. As the disturbed person paints, it usually comes about that he gives expression to conflicts within his mind. So I encourage the patient to talk to me in a very relaxed way about the things he has painted and by this means I learn something of his inner problem. On many occasions patients have painted patterns exactly like the stylized tulips which ornament the mosques. Without knowing what he was doing the patient has given symbols, he frequently starts telling me of sexual problems that are related to his illness.

Are we to think from this that the purity of holy places has been defiled by symbols of sex? No, this is not defilement. It is an expression of the nature of man. I have spoken of the lingam of the Hindus, and the stylized representation of the Tibetan Buddha in sexual congress with the beautiful Tara. God, Creation and Sex are ideas that are inexorably interwoven. And it is this that adds to the wonder of it all.

And Christianity. Do these things apply here too? Of course they do, and it is natural that they should. Just one little example. For centuries the Annunciation has been a favourite subject for painters. The angel Gabriel is shown telling the Virgin that she will bear a child. It has become a tradition that the angel is represented as holding a staff or a lily in his hand. This of course is a sexual symbol unconsciously denoting the sexual nature of the visitation. In fact this sexual symbol, the lily, has become the recognized emblem of the Virgin.

A Visit to the Caspian Sea

When I arrived back in Tehran I had a little time to spare, so I hired a car and driver and set off for the Caspian Sea. It was incredibly hot. The road rose and twisted through high mountains. The sun poured down into the airless pass. Then at last we descended to the apparently tropical country of the Caspian seaboard.

I had seen tourist posters of the fashionable beach resorts of the Caspian Sea. So we went there first with the idea of cooling down with a swim. But the tourist posters had not shown that the sand was nearly black, nor that the water was murky and so warm as to be enervating. And I thought of the Australian beaches with their clear, cool water, and the mile upon mile of shining white sand. And the other bathers were so different from those of the Australian beaches. These people were all fat, men, women and children, all of them. Then I began to understand it. These were wealthy people. In Persia it is only the wealthy who can drive down to the beach for a swim. Old traditions and customs still continue. In a country of great poverty, where some still starve and many have scarcely enough to eat, it remains fashionable to be fat. This is an external sign of wealth and position. It is the age-old status symbol of Persia. But we, in my country, are not without our status symbols too. One of them is not to appear fat on the beaches, but to appear fit. This is our cult. Boys and girls, men and women, want their friends to say, 'How fit you look!' And of course to look fit you must be sun-tanned. So we lie in the sun, all of us, our skin is bronzed and we look fit. But not so the Persians. I soon noticed this. They are a relatively light-skinned race. They are proud of this, so they have no desire to tan their skin to a darker shade. Their aim is to appear on the beach with a body that is fat and white.

After lunch we commenced the drive back to Tehran. The heat was now past the ordinary discomfort of a very hot day. To me it was quite alarming. We drove on for an hour or so without speaking. We were now in the pass through the high mountains, the bare rocks gave back their heat into the stagnant air. Then the car started to weave from one side of the road to the other. I looked at the driver. His eyes were half shut. I nudged him and spoke to him, but he made no sensible reply. I managed to get him to stop the car. This was the beginning of heat-stroke. We were miles from anywhere. Fortunately the road was following a mountain stream up the pass. I half dragged the befuddled driver to the edge of the stream. I quickly took off my clothes, and helped him to do the same. Then I got him into the water, and in a few moments he was right again.

Not far from the scene of this little adventure is the location of one of the most remarkable archaelogical discoveries of recent times. This is the discovery of the Luristan bronzes. This has all happened in the last thirty years. I have two or three small pieces. What the real meaning of them is I do not know. And various attempts to find out have not helped me. But this I do know; there is magic about them. There is a recurrent theme of a human figure between two rearing beasts. but these are sometimes so distorted for decorative purposes that neither the figure nor the animals are recognizable as such. It is all embellished with other animals. Sometimes these are elongated and stylized to make an intricate pattern so that the shape of one animal merges into another. There is great art here, and there has been great skill in casting these pieces. This I can understand, but the meaning of it for a long time completely eluded me. But now I think I understand just something of it. These things have a fairly constant form. There is the central figure and the two beasts rearing on either side. It is the same shape again as the stylized tulips on the mosques and the lingam of the Hindu temples. But I am sure that this is only part of the story. The rest remains hidden in the darkness of time. But I like my Luristan bronze. It sits on my desk and beside it there is a Luristan clay animal. He is the strangest animal I have ever seen. He might be a lion. I believe that he has spent nearly three thousand years at the side of his former master. He was there to protect him. Now he is here to do the same for me; and I feel that he does it very well.

A Glimpse of Child Labour

I have a liking for Persian carpets, so I asked if I could see them being made. I was driven to a small village some distance from the city. Then through strange gates in high walls, through another door and I was suddenly met with the babble of children's voices. Rarely have I been so surprised. A carpet hung vertically from the ceiling. On either side of it there were two or three planks supported between trestles such as painters use. On the planks were seated little children, boys and girls, aged five, six and seven, some perhaps even younger. Child labour, and such little children! As I came in they all stopped work and started calling to me, stretching out their hands for me to give them something. Some clambered down from the planks on which they worked. The man in charge quickly shooed them back. They obeyed promptly but I saw no fear in them. In fact they were all smiling and happy with big brown eyes and white teeth. Perhaps it was that my visit had brought a temporary respite from the day's drudgery and with it just a moment or two of happiness. I do not know. Then they started work again, knotting little pieces of wool into the intricate pattern of the carpet. Two or three older girls of twelve or fourteen supervised the younger ones. One of them indicated that I should try. I knew what it would be, but I thought I should not deny them a laugh. I was all fingers and thumbs, and the youngest of them laughed loudest of all.

On the way out I was led past a shed where women were baking. I stopped and watched them. The ground-up grain was mixed into a dough. This was taken in the hand and plastered on to hot bricks heated by a fire underneath. It was soon baked, thin and crisp, about the size of a plate. The women smiled and offered me some. Like the children working on the carpet they were happy and friendly.

It appears that carpet-making is a village enterprise. The men and some women work in the fields, other women bake and prepare food, and the young children are set to work in the traditional fashion making the carpets that I like so much.

As I drove back I thought perhaps I did not like Persian carpets quite so much. But I did not want to lose my liking for them, and I kept reminding myself that the children had seemed perfectly happy. Perhaps it is like other things; if we know too much about their origin we lose our taste for them. We like meat, but less so if at meal time we think too much about the animal that provided it.

Trick or Supernatural

Bangkok is a stopping place on the flight from Australia to
Europe, and on a number of occasions I have broken my journey there. On these visits I have come to know a Thai psychiatrist whom I now regard as a friend. Like most Buddhists,
he is a quiet, sincere, humble man. On one occasion he asked
if he could demonstrate a strange phenomenon with a patient
whom he had been treating with hypnosis. The patient was a
Thai lad of eighteen who could speak no English. There were
two or three other doctors present at the demonstration and
several assistants. My friend introduced me and asked the
patient to sit on a chair. He then hypnotized the patient. This
was simple enough as it had been done many times before. His
head sagged as it often does in hypnosis; and his eyes rolled
upwards and back so that there was only the white showing
before they settled down again in the normal position. My
friend then proceeded to blindfold the lad. First he covered his
eyes with a wide strip of elastoplast. Then he packed cotton
wool tightly over each eye where the elastoplast was held off
the skin by the projection of the nose. Then he tied a thick
towel around his head completely covering his eyes. I was
quite convinced that the lad was totally blindfold. My friend
made sure that he was still hypnotized. He then placed a pencil
in his hand and some paper in front of him. I was given a
pack of cards, and was asked to hold a card in front of the
blindfold subject. I did this. I remember it was the five of
hearts. Then the lad rather shakily wrote down the figure 5
and drew after it a heart. I was quite amazed. The experiment was repeated two or three times with the same result.
I noticed that sometimes he moved his head about a little, but
I do not believe that he could have peeped under the elastoplast because this area had been tightly packed with cotton
wool. It was very hot, and we had all taken off our jackets; so
next time we repeated the experiment I held my jacket between
the lad's face and the card. This seemed to disturb him, and

rather than persist with it, the experiment was discontinued. My friend untied the towel. The elastoplast and cotton wool were all in place, completely covering his eyes. When these were then taken off, it could be seen that the lad was still in a deep trance. He was awakened by my friend. He was a little bewildered for a moment, and then spoke quite normally with the Thai doctors.

The only explanation that I could give was that my friend saw the card, and the hypnotized patient became aware of it by telepathy. I mentioned earlier that I myself on two occasions have had what would seem to be indisputable evidence of telepathic communication with deeply hypnotized patients. It seems that hostile or disturbing influences will prevent telepathy. This appeared to be so when I tried to repeat my own experience with an observer in the room. My holding of the coat between the lad and the card may have had this type of effect. When they had finished I could think of all the interesting experiments which would have proved the matter one way or the other. But my plane would not wait for me, and I had to be off.

On another visit to Bangkok my psychiatrist friend told me of a very devout Buddhist friend of his who is credited with the power of clairvoyance. It was arranged that I should meet him. However at the last minute he changed his mind and declined to see me. He is a very religious young man, and I gather that he rather regards his power as part of religious experience, and for this reason he does not wish to be investigated scientifically. However, on occasions he will use his gift to help people in trouble. Quite recently another friend of the Thai psychiatrist had had his car stolen. So they consulted the clairvoyant Buddhist about it to see if he could offer any advice. He agreed to help. He let himself go into a deep trance, and then told the owner of the car to look in a certain street. He did so, and the car was there.

This of course is a second-hand story. I was not a witness of the incident, but I feel that I could vouch for the integrity of my psychiatrist friend.

These matters lie on the very fringe of human knowledge. We know very little about them. But why don't we look and see, and try to find out? The fact is that scientists are very chary of investigating such matters. I know this to be true from my own personal experience in investigating hypnosis.

Scientists have to be thought scientific. Even in these days mediæval attitudes of mind persist, and anyone who investigates telepathy or clairvoyance is likely to be thought a little queer himself.

In an attempt to follow up these matters I recently spent some time with a world famous Western clairvoyant. He actually prefers to be known as a paragnost. Before my meeting with him I had read about some of his work in a scientific journal. On a number of occasions he had been able to help the police to find the bodies of murdered persons. In a controlled experiment he had described the person who would sit in a certain seat in a theatre some days before the performance, and it was subsequently proved that at the time of this prognostication the person in question had not even bought the ticket. I remembered the deep serenity of some of the yogi mystics who had claimed similar powers. So I went to meet the clairvoyant with the expectation of meeting a very superior person. But I was immediately disappointed. As a man he was conspicuously ordinary. He apparently had had little formal education. I am sure he was well below average in intelligence; and most striking of all, he had the jitters. He said that he suffered from nervous indigestion. We had a meal together. He would only eat raw eggs. Then he immediately developed severe indigestion, and for some time kept groaning, and holding his hand on his stomach. It all seemed so incongruous in a man who was renowned for his mental abilities.

He was a man in his mid-forties. He explained that he had been able to see visions since an early age, and these could often be used to find missing objects or the bodies of murdered persons, particularly children. He regarded the visions as God-given, and would not discuss their origin further than this. In response to my questions he firmly denied that he ever went into a trance or reverie when seeing the visions. He said that he often saw his best visions when someone called him on the telephone and sought his help about some missing object or person. On these occasions the vision would often come immediately and he would see the missing object in its surroundings.

A husband and wife, who had lost their only child, a boy of fourteen, some eighteen months previously, had heard of the clairvoyant's visit to the city, and had asked if they could speak with him and seek his help. They had never seen the clairvoyant before. He listened to their story. Then when they had finished, he wriggled about uncomfortably on his chair for a moment, and asked, 'Is there a building like a barracks near where you live?'

'There are no barracks. But there is a block of flats that could look like a barracks.'

'Is there a water-tower nearby?'

'Yes, there is.'

'Is the top of it green?'

'I don't know, but it could be.'

'Is there a tram-stop or bus-stop there?'

'Yes.'

'Your boy took the bus there. Is there water near where you live, an inlet or a river?'

'Yes, within four or five miles.'

Then he said, 'You must find a little jetty. It has some broken boards at the end. There is a man there who hires out boats. Ask him if he lost a green boat on the day your son was lost.'

He then seemed to be rather disturbed and motioned for the couple to leave him. I thought that he had had a recurrence of his indigestion, but when the couple had left, he explained that he had seen something to do with a homosexual assault, and he did not wish to distress the parents further by disclosing this to them.

I was left with a feeling of bewilderment and wonder. Why can't we investigate these matters properly?

In a Monastery Garden

In Thailand every male Buddhist must spend a period of three months in a monastery. This is usually done when the boy is sixteen or seventeen years old. However, a man may serve his three months at any time of his life. My psychiatrist friend took me to visit a relative, a man in his middle forties. He was a doctor in the Thai navy, and at this stage of his life had elected to spend three months in the monastery. We talked together in the garden. He spoke good English, and I soon found myself at ease with him. It was the old story again. He was calm and relaxed, and in a few minutes I too felt it. He had unconsciously communicated something to me.

This of course is what I try to do every day in my consulting room. I feel that this is something which should become much more a part of our everyday living in our ordinary contacts with our fellows. If we could remember this, or better still, if we could let it become a habit, life would become very much easier and more pleasant.

He had been in the monastery for some two months, and said he felt much better for it. But was this due to escape from the immediate stress of his work, or was it due to something else? He thought both factors came into it; and he believed that much of what he gained in the monastery would remain with him afterwards. He was quite frank. He was not accustomed to a cloistered life, and he found certain aspects of monastic discipline irksome. One of them, as I understood it, was that he was required to take off his sandals, not only in the presence of one of the monks, but even if a monk walked past him. A few minutes later this situation arose while I was talking with him. He complied with the regulation with an air of calm humility, and no outward sign of disquiet.

I commented that three months off work would be quite a financial burden for some people. But no. In Thailand the salaries of all those who work for the government are continued during their monastic retreat. People in the West say, 'What a waste of government money.' But I wonder if it is. If government is something that leads people to a happy and contented life, then this should be a normal part of government expenditure. But the idea is foreign to our way of life and materialistic standards of value.

The monasteries call on the Buddhist youth at approximately the same time as our boys are called to military service. From my practice of psychiatry I know that many young people in this age group go through a period of active idealism. I see this professionally in many young university students. Their idealism finds expression in different ways. There are outward manifestations such as enlisting in the peace corps, demands for civil rights, protests against injustice, war and violence. But very many young people, who never express their idealism in outward form, are in fact subject to very considerable idealistic preoccupation. They seldom talk of it, and it is really only the psychiatrist who becomes familiar with it as he explores their inner thoughts. The point, of course, is that in Buddhist countries these young people are exposed to a profound religious and spiritual influence just at that period in their lives when they are best suited for it. Whereas our youth is so often subjected to military call-up and camp-life influences which promptly extinguish the flame of early idealism.

Youth is the age of idealism, but to many of us there comes a second period of idealistic thought and endeavour. This commonly comes in middle age. And again, I have my experience as a psychiatrist to substantiate this observation. In this later period there is generally less fire, and less of the burning desire to put things right. Rather it is a matter of trying to achieve an inner understanding. I felt that this was the case with my doctor friend in the monastery.

In Eastern countries this reawakening of idealism in later life is accepted as a natural occurrence. In India when a man's children have grown to relative independence, it is not uncommon for the father to leave home and devote himself, temporarily or permanently, to the spiritual life. In Western culture we see expressions of this need in organizations like Rotary and Freemasonry. In one culture the drive for idealism is satisfied in a personal isolation and contemplation; in the other by material giving, and by an active sense of fellowship as is the custom in our way of life.

The Clash of Cultures

The Thais are nice people. This may seem a silly statement; but I believe it to be true. The typical Thai has a type of personality different from the typical Westerner, whether he be American, British, European or Australian. The outstanding features are his calm and his lack of aggression. The typical Western male is really pretty tense and quite aggressive. By 'aggressive' I mean a desire to assert himself, both over those who are about him, and his environment in general. The Thai has little of this. As a result we get the feeling that we are talking to a mature woman rather than a man. Don't let me confuse you with thoughts of the bustling American woman, who talks everyone down and who always knows best. No. This is not psychological maturity, but a perverted twist of the feminine personality towards the masculine type. No. I refer rather to the mature woman who expresses the fullness of her femininity by being passive. She runs her family, manages her husband and gains her ends by bringing things about passively. As she is passive there is calm about her. Because of this natural calm we feel it good to be with her, we feel comfortable talking to her. So it is with a Thai.

I believe that this is true of the native Thai who has had little contact with Western influences. But during the ten or twelve years which span my visits, there have been great changes in Thailand, especially in Bangkok itself. You all know the story. You can see it all through South-East Asia. It is the story of how much we Westerners are doing for these people, but at the same time how we are destroying their souls. It is all very strange. It is all very sad. We are trying to do our best, but we don't understand. We bring them food when they are starving; we save their lives with modern drugs and surgery; we teach them to read and write and thus open up the storehouse of Western knowledge. We do all this, but we have not been able to give them any adequate stabilizing influence to replace what we have destroyed in bringing them these wonderful things. They see us as strong and wise. They want to be like us, particularly the younger ones. We pay no respect to their temples and their gods, so why should they. We show them our way of life in films and TV; and like children they try to copy it. For generations children have followed their parents' way of life, but now they leave home to work in the industry which we have brought them. The guiding force of parents and village elders has gone; and we make no attempt to put anything in its place. My psychiatric friend works with young people, and each time I see him he speaks of the still greater increase in juvenile crime and delinquency.

The young Thai who has grown up under our influence has lost these gracious qualities of which I speak. He is like us. Given a truck to drive, he has his hand on the horn, and he scatters the villagers, women and children, as he participates in this new way of life.

But it is not only the Thais who suffer. We do ourselves. In the first intermingling of cultures both sides gain. We use their labour; they learn our techniques. But in another way both sides lose. Let us not forget how often the Westerner in the East deteriorates. The climate, alcohol, women, all play a part; but above all there is a loss of personal standards. The reality of this is obvious to any visitor. On a grand scale it was demonstrated in the war by lack of morale of the white population of Singapore when faced by the Japanese.

It seems that the treatment can be as bad as the disease. And this is true of our approach to other things. And I shall speak of psychiatry because this is what I know most about. I have seen many who have been cured, but who would still drive through the village with their hand on the horn. But there are some who are treated by others who can drive where they could not drive before, and who may even give the woman and her child a lift on the way.

7 MEXICO

The Mayas

I went down to Merida in the Yucatan peninsula to see something of the Maya remains. It is hot, flat, infertile country covered with low scrub. I could not help wondering why the Mayas had chosen such a place to build their cities when there are so many more attractive sites. But things may have changed. It is between a thousand and fifteen hundred years since the Mayas built their temples and public buildings at Chichen-Itza. In Aden, at the mouth of the Red Sea, I remember being shown ancient reservoirs and irrigation schemes which have remained dry during the living memory of man; yet clear water-marks show that at some time in the past there was sufficient rain to fill the dams. There may have been some similar change of climate at the site of the Maya civilization.

There are huge pyramids. But they are different from the pyramids of Egypt. These were built as tombs of great rulers, whereas the Mayan pyramids were places for religious rites. Unlike the Egyptian pyramids which taper to a point, the Mayan variety have a flat top. It was here that the priests performed their rituals, and the greatest ritual of all was human sacrifice.

In human sacrifice the Mayas were no match for the Aztecs who had their centre of government at the site where Mexico City now stands, and who were at the height of their power at the time of the Spanish conquest. For cruelty they remain unsurpassed. It is estimated that in a single year twenty thousand living people had their hearts cut out. And it was all done in the name of their gods. The Spanish record the stench of the place, and the beating of the great gong that drowned the shrieks of the victims. Cortes and his men put an end to all this but in doing so they displayed a reckless savagery that almost equalled that of the Aztecs themselves. And this too was in the name of God. The Spaniards, driven by a thirst for loot and a frenzy of religious zeal completely destroyed the city. Golden ritual vessels were smuggled away, and the temple itself torn down, and in its place now stands the cathedral.

But in the Yucatan the Maya remains have been left, and we can see them as a monument of one of the strangest digressions in man's march of progress. I stood by the great pyramid, and let my mind people the bare steps with the pageant of the past. Here the victim, bedecked for the occasion, was stretched over the stone to have his heart cut out. And this to be done so quickly, so skilfully that the bloody organ would be in the hands of the high priest while it was still beating. Here was the gutter that drained away his blood. And I had seen the knives that were used. They had no iron or bronze to make a metal knife. These people knew only the soft metals, gold and silver. The heart was ripped from the victim with a stone knife about a foot long and some three inches wide. As a doctor I found it hard to imagine how they did it. On some occasions the victim was immediately skinned, and while still hot, his skin was sewn over the high priest. Then, decked in the strange array, he performed a ritual dance.

Why did they do these things? I do not know. But I can guess. They did it to propitiate the rain god, Chac. But there was more to it than this. The priests did these things to preserve their own power. This seems to be part of the natural history of ritual. We develop some magical act to try to bring about something which we do not understand. We would like to believe that it works. We come to think that it does work. Then we become afraid not to continue the ritual. The one who performs the ritual thus has powers over his fellows. Because of his power he fears that others will seize his position. So he makes the ritual more and more complicated so that he cannot be replaced. I think you could trace this process in the development of ritual of some branches of the Christian church. A priesthood which could develop such a terrible ritual as ripping the heart from the living man would be all the more secure by reason of the horror of it.

A little distance from the great pyramid there is the court in which they played their own special type of ball game. It is a walled court, rectangular, and several times the size of a tennis court. The game was played like basket-ball except that the players were not allowed to touch the ball with their hands. It was evidently something like soccer. On either side of the court there is a projecting ring of stone work, but unlike the rings for basket-ball, these are in a vertical position. The objective was to get the ball through the ring. Apparently the game might continue for days. Finally the losing team was disgraced and the winners were accorded every licence.

Near Taxco I have seen the remains of a much smaller court. This was used in later times for the Aztec version of the Mayan ball game. As in other things the Aztecs brought their bloody rituals into the game. This was a game of singles. The story is that the loser was utterly disgraced and enslaved for ever. The winner on the other hand was accorded every honour, and in the moment of triumph and ecstasy, he was offered to the gods at the temple, and his heart was cut out.

A Sacred Well

A short walk from these ruins there is the sacred well, the cenote of Chichen-Itza. The terrain of the Yucatan is of lime-stone, and under this there is a high water table. In various places there are holes, or cenotes, in the rock, which lead down to this water and so form natural wells. These were a source of water in Maya times just as they are today. The sacred well at Chichen-Itza is a very large cenote some one hundred and fifty to two hundred feet in diameter with murky water in its depths. In 1905 it was dredged by archaeologists and many remarkable gold and silver objects were recovered. The site remains untouched. There is just the water-hole and a few trees nearby. It was all very peaceful. At the edge of the well there are the ruins of a small room.

Here, in times of crises, human offerings were made to the great god, Chac. It must have seemed appropriate to all that the god of rain should be propitated at such a mysterious source of water. The story is that a chosen virgin was bedecked with golden ornaments which would ensure that she would sink and thus be accepted by the god. With due ceremony she was taken to the priest in the little room at the edge of the well. Here her final preparation was completed, and she was cast into the well.

On other occasions valuable articles were thrown into the well as offerings without the additional human sacrifice.

At other times the cenote was used to discover the pleasure of the god. Slave girls were thrown into the well in the early morning. The people then left the well. At midday they returned and threw in a rope; if any girl survived, she was able to interpret the will of the god.

I sat in the ruins of the little room where the girls had experienced their final preparations by the priest. All through history and in vastly different cultures there has been a strange relationship between the priests and the virgins who attended the temples. We have only to think of the cults of ancient Egypt or the Vestal Virgins of classical antiquity.

In travel we come upon many strange customs. These are interesting in themselves; but it is of far greater interest to note the way in which these strange customs are so often repeated in some unexpected aspect of our own everyday life. I can recollect having had as patients four different women who had been seduced by priests. Of these two were Catholic and two Protestant. The point that I would wish to make is that none of these was an ordinary act of unchastity. In each case the women regarded the event as something in the way of mystical union. They were all rather conscientious women and did not experience the usual feelings of guilt which would be expected in such circumstances. Two of them were quite intensely religious women, and claimed that their sense of religious well-being had increased as a result of these experiences. There is no doubt that many strange ideas are hidden deep in the minds of many apparently normal people.

Guadalupe

On both sides of his ancestry, from Aztecs and the Spaniards, the Mexican has a heritage of religious fervour. It is seen in the creole whose Spanish blood is untainted; in the pure Indian; and in the Mestizo of mixed blood.

On my first visit to Mexico I joined a tourist group to visit Guadalupe which is a little distance from the centre of Mexico City.

On the hill nearby in 1521 the Virgin appeared to an Indian peasant named Jaun Diego. In fact she appeared to him on several occasions. She was clad in traditional robes, but she herself was dark in colour like an Indian. She told him to tell the Bishop of her visitation, but he was frightened and asked her for a sign. He was told to pick some wildflowers, put them in his cape and take them to the Bishop. He did this; and when he unfolded his cape there was painted on it a beautiful picture of the Virgin, brown-skinned, as he had seen her. She became known as 'La Morena', and quickly became worshipped throughout Mexico, so that pictures of La Morena are now to be seen everywhere that one goes throughout the country.

I myself know several people who have seen visions of the Virgin. I mention this only as a matter of interest and not in any attempt to discredit La Morena. Those whom I know who have seen visions have all shown clear-cut signs of mental illness. Most of them when they have recovered have realized that their vision was a result of the disorder of their mind at the time. However two or three of these patients have recovered and have resumed a normal life, but the belief in the genuine nature of the vision has remained with them.

The rapid spread of the worship of La Morena was, of course, due to her dark skinned appearance. This was a breakthrough for the native Indians. Both Cortes and the bishop were aware of the significance of the situation to Indians, and they supported the movement; but for a long time it was opposed by the Franciscan monks.

In front of the church there is a large forecourt. All day and well into the night across this square there is a long line of pilgrims. But they do not walk quietly to the church as one might expect, they go on their knees. At the edge of the square most of the pilgrims, men, women and children, drop on their knees, and make uncomfortable progress across the stones of the square, up the steps and down the aisle of the church.

I arrived there with my group of tourists. It was horrible walking with a loud-mouthed guide among these kneeling pilgrims. I could not stand it. I broke off from the party. But I had seen enough to make me want to see more. So later that afternoon I went back there by myself. I paid off my taxi, and I was there with the pilgrims. It was dusk and very still. There were no tourists now. Although I was not going to the church as an act of faith, I was greatly moved by those who were. I watched them quietly. Not one of them looked in my direction. They were far too occupied with thoughts of other things to even notice me. I walked along the line, slowly and thoughtfully, to the steps of the church. For some time I stood there in reverie. It was growing dark outside, and the light of the lamps and the candles lit up their faces as they approached the door. It is hard to walk up stone steps on one's knees. And their knees were sore from their long progress across the square. Some were bleeding. I quietly studied their faces. It was clear that some were in quite an unusual state of consciousness. They gazed ahead fixedly. I am sure they had little awareness of other pilgrims only a few feet from them, or of me and two or three others standing on the steps. They showed no signs of pain which in normal circumstances would have been considerable. They did not look about them; in fact they seemed quite oblivious of their surroundings. According to my standards many of them were clearly in a trance. For some time I watched and wondered about it all. Then I went inside. The church was crowded, but luckily there was a place by the aisle on the back pew. I sat there watching the procession file past me to the altar.

I thought they were mainly mixed blooded Mestizos, there were Indians and also those who appeared to be of pure European blood. Some were well dressed; some in rags. There were many men, although women and children predominated. Many were obviously ill. Some of them were supported by friends kneeling on either side of them.

Here there were pathos and hope. And I thought of faces I had seen in the out-patients hall of the public hospital where I once worked. Then the faces I had seen in an Indian hospital came to me. And I realized more than ever that true medicine can never be the pure technology which is being taught more and more in our medical schools.

I was in no hurry to leave. It was dark when I walked back across the square, but there were still a few starting their pilgrimage to the church.

I waited there in the dark before seeking a taxi. What did it all mean? There was no full answer. But certain things came to me. These people had a burning need of something. And this need is satisfied or partially satisfied in what I had seen. It came to me, clearly and forcefully, that these people were the better for this experience, as even I myself was from my participation from the periphery. This much seemed clear. But are there similar people in our own community who are in need of something like this? Do you and I have such a need which we do not acknowledge? Or is it that people in our community do not have this need? Maybe not. We are more sophisticated, and that may do away with such a need. Or is it that the same need in our community is satisfied in other ways? I can ask more questions than I can answer. Are people like me, the psychiatrists, to become the priests of the new world? If so we must be given very different training from what we are given at present.

Many of those who toil across the square on their knees are tense, or depressed, or have some physical ailment which may be either psychosomatic or organic in origin. In our community such people see the local doctor. The chances are that they will be given tranquillizing or antidepressant drugs. This undoubtedly helps them to feel better. Maybe they have to come back for more drugs. But they carry on. Just as the people I saw that night can carry on as a result of their experience at the church. In both cases it is the reduction of anxiety that counts. But life cannot be judged simply by one's ability to keep going. There are qualities of living. Perhaps for those who make the pilgrimage to La Morena, whether they be in rags and illiterate or not, life is of a different quality from those who control their anxiety by taking tranquillizing tablets.

Cusco

I was going to Rio de Janeiro to attend an international meeting about the use of hypnosis in medicine. So I thought I should see what I could of South America.

I wanted to see something of the Inca remains, so I took a plane from Lima to Cusco. This was quite an adventure in itself. Cusco, the ancient Inca capital, is situated up in the Andes at 11,500 feet above sea level. To get there the plane has to fly at some 20,000 feet in order to cross the main mass of the Andes. This does not seem very difficult. But the plane was not pressurized! Things happen slowly in South America. Oxygen was provided by pipes to the seats. Each passenger had a little rubber tube with a plastic nozzle, which he was instructed to hold in his mouth. There were two very efficient air-hostesses who carried small cylinders of oxygen in smart little bags slung over their shoulders with a rubber tube attached. They had developed the knack of holding the nozzle of the tube between their teeth and talking at the same time. By this means they kept their hands free to do whatever had to be done. This was rather in the way some men talk without taking their pipe from their mouth.

We were soon told to use the oxygen. I noticed that the man sitting in the seat immediately in front of me did not do so. He was a big, strong fellow. By his manner he gave everyone the impression that he had made the trip many times before, and that this oxygen stuff may be all right for women and children, but was quite unnecessary for a he-man like himself. His manner was sufficiently unusual to draw attention to himself. The young hostesses were busy explaining things to some rather frightened old ladies. The man then stood up, and started to parade up and down the aisle. It was now obvious to everyone that he was quite queer. The two hostesses immediately left the old ladies, and made a dash after him. Very quickly and very effectively they manhandled him back to his seat, pushed him down into it, and half sitting on top of him, held the oxygen tube in his mouth. All this happened so quickly that there was no commotion from the other passengers who hardly realized what was going on. In a moment or two he was perfectly all right. I thought, 'Full marks to the Peruvian air-hostesses.'

One of the greatest dangers in lack of oxygen is the fact that the individual is not aware of it. The man on the plane demonstrated this point beautifully, as he was quite unaware that he was acting strangely or that anything at all was wrong with him.

On arrival at Cusco we were warned to walk slowly, and not to over-exert ourselves until we had become accustomed to the rarefied air at 11,500 feet.

The next day I hired a car and amid magnificent scenery was driven farther up the mountains to over 13,000 feet. On these highlands I saw llamas grazing. These strange animals seem to provide all the needs of the mountain folk of these regions, milk, meat and wool, and in addition to this they act as beasts of burden.

At a turn in the road we came upon quite a remarkable sight. There was a little boy not far distant sitting on a large stone playing a pipe as he watched over a few llamas. I asked the driver to stop so that I could listen. The boy stopped playing and looked at us, and then continued again. I then walked over to him. He must have been about ten or twelve. He was clad literally in rags of rough cloth made from llama wool. I motioned him to play more. Here was a replica of the Greek shepherd boy of classical times minding his flock on Mount Olympus and playing his pipe to pass the time of day.

On the side of the mountain overlooking Cusco there are the remains of an Inca temple. It was destroyed by the Spaniards who took the stone to build the Christian counter-part, which I could see far below me in the city square. There remains a semi-circle of great stone seats, or perhaps it would be better to describe them as rough thrones. When the king of the Incas died his body was embalmed. At meetings of the council of state the mummified bodies of previous Inca kings were placed on these thrones to watch over the deliberations of the present king and his council. Now the grass was growing all about it, and llamas grazed among the stones. It was still, and as I wandered about this strange place the ghosts of the past were hovering close at hand. Then I heard the cathedral bell echoing up the mountain. And I stood there a long time looking down on the city from where the sound was coming.

From this sanctuary on the mountain the Inca looked down on the city as I was doing now. When making important decisions, it seems that he knew the value of separating himself from the bustle of the market place and those concerned with it. With these strange reminders of the past beside him he would be ever mindful of the experience of those who had gone before.

The Lost City of the Incas

Many an ancient city has been sacked and destroyed and left deserted. Dirt and sand have blown over the ruins, and in the course of time knowledge as to the exact site of the city has been lost. The once great city of Troy is an example of this process, and there are many others. But Machu Picchu, the lost city of the Incas, is quite different. It was never sacked or destroyed. It was just lost to the rest of the world. And this happened in quite recent times. It must surely be one of the strangest stories in history. But this was high up in the Andes and strange things happen there.

Pizarro took Cusco, and the Inca king was held captive. Then after exacting a huge ransom he had the Inca killed. This was in 1533. There was great loot in gold, but at the same time there seems to have been a suggestion that some of the treasures were taken from the city before the arrival of the Spaniards. And one of the Spanish priests in his chronicle suggests that some of the Inca priests may have escaped. There were vague rumours of an Inca city in the jungle which had never been found. With no more reliable information than this on which he could depend, an American archaeologist Hiram Bingham, set out to investigate the rumours of a lost city in the Andes. He made contact with various Indians in the jungle, and within the limits of communication sought information about any ruins. In extremely difficult mountain country he was directed hither and thither, only to find an occasional Inca stone or two. He began to suspect that the Indians might be purposely misdirecting him. After months of fruitless search he was on the point of abandoning the project

Then some Indians directed him up a high mountain with almost vertical walls. He decided that this would be his last attempt. He scaled the mountain, and there at the top, covered with jungle growth, were the ruins of Machu Picchu. This was in 1911.

The jungle has now been cleared away and the visitor can explore the ruins. It is really a fabulous place. It is built on the top of a mountain which is in the hairpin bend of a river so that on three sides the walls are almost vertical. On the remaining side there is an easily defended razor-back ridge connecting it with the mountain range.

It was a beautiful day of clear sunshine. Wisps of mist floated in the valley beneath. There was an eerie stillness. We seemed to be floating on the mist.

Archaeologists have searched the area and found graves. But strangest of all, the skeletons are nearly all those of women.

The mists linger about Machu Picchu and there is no clear light on the history of this strange place. The story as pieced together, seems to be that Incas had word of the approach of the Spaniards. In order to preserve the sacred relics the Inca king sent them to Machu Picchu with priests and virgins so that their sacred rites might be continued, in spite of anything that might happen to the Inca himself at the hands of the Spaniards. It is not known how long this continued, or how it all finished. It seems that the end came peacefully. Perhaps they just died off, and the last few abandoned their holy task, and left their city on the mountain to mingle their blood with tribesmen of the jungle around them.

To Let the Devil out of the Head

I returned to Lima and found there a most interesting museum. The long narrow strip of land between the Andes on the east and the Pacific on the west is excessively dry. There is in fact one place which boasts that it has never been known to rain there. This extremely dry atmosphere had led to the preservation of early relics in quite an extraordinary way, just as the dry climate of Egypt helped to preserve the contents of the tombs of Ancient Egypt.

There are pottery utensils that go back to early Christian

times. But it was a number of skulls which intrigued me. They
had little square holes cut in them, about half an inch in
diameter. This was done to let out the devil or bad spirit which
had been giving the individual such a bad headache. Some of
the instruments were displayed which had been used to trefine
skulls in this way. They were made of bronze, shaped so that
the cutting edge was curved. These were rubbed back and
forth on the patient's head until a linear cut was made through
the bone. Then a similar cut was made parallel to the first
and about half an inch away. Two more cuts at right angles
isolated a little square of bone. This was then removed with
the help of a little hook which was attached to the handle of
the bronze cutting instrument. And even more interesting, the
bone of some of the skulls had grown over in the healing process. This was definite proof that the patient had lived for
some time after the operation.

The next day I was wandering around Lima and by accident
I came upon an antiquarian shop. I fell into conversation with
another customer who disclosed that he was buying for one of
the great museums of Europe. He convinced me that the things
on display were in fact genuine. Among a pile of encrusted
bronze tools I found two instruments which were apparently
used for trefining skulls. I bought these thinking they would
be a good present for a neuro-surgeon friend of mine. But I
have become attached to these relics of the doctor's art of
another age; and I have never given them to my friend. Instead they remain on the mantelshelf in my consulting-room.
I see many neurotic patients complaining of headache. I often
have some trouble in talking the devil or evil spirits out of
their heads. Sometimes I think it might be a good plan to
resort to the more direct methods of my pre-Inca medical colleagues.

But it is not only the modern neuro-surgeons who drill holes
in the skull to relieve headache. The practice still persists with
some primitive peoples. Last year I met a doctor, whose name
eludes me, who had photographs of Rhodesian natives who
had their skulls trefined by witch-doctors. In each case the
photographs disclosed a large abscess following the operation.
Nevertheless, remarkably enough, the patients still lived. There
was one photograph of a patient who had gone back for a
second operation. This I thought was further proof of two
things which are a constant cause of wonder to me. That there

are so very many different forms of medical treatment which all help to relieve the neurotic patient, even though some forms work better than others. And man, whether primitive or sophisticated, seems to have a blind and unnatural faith in his medical attendant, whether witch-doctor or neuro-surgeon. You can see how this is a danger that might destroy the patient; but I can see it as a danger that can destroy the doctor himself.

9 BRAZIL

A Medical Meeting in Rio

In one way or another international medical meetings seem
to take on some aspect of the national character of the country
in which they are held. I have been to quite a few now, and
it always seems to be the same. Sometimes there is an air of
social gathering. Sometimes the important thing seems to be
that it is all a tax deduction. At others, people quietly get on
with the serious business of the meeting. But at Rio it was
different again. There were flags and a brass band, and even
more unexpected, I found myself seated on the dais next to
the minister for the navy. This was at a meeting on hypnosis.
There were other ministers and important people also present.
In fact the president himself had been scheduled to open the
congress, but was unable to come at the last minute.

My children, in the way that many children feel about their
parents, have at times claimed that I am slow witted and lacking in humour. But they would have had no doubts about me
this day at Rio. It all seemed so ridiculously incongruous that
I could hardly keep a straight face.

But I gradually came to understand. We laugh too readily
at those who do not do things just the same way as we do.
Here in Rio, status is very important. Somehow or other, I
don't just quite understand why, but it gives status to have
a minister of state sit next to you at a medical meeting on
hypnosis.

The next few days showed me how really significant status
can be in the lives of people. For the local practitioners it was
very important to read a paper at the meeting. As a result
hundreds of papers were offered as status symbols for the individuals, and not because they had anything new to say. Because of the status element, any criticism of technical aspect
of a paper was immediately taken as an affront to the individual. When status has reached this exaggerated form, I could
find it hard to imagine anyone saying that he was not sure, or
that he did not know, or that he had a failure. Yet I recently

attended a meeting in another country where most of the discussion centred around an open admission of failures in the hope that others would not make the same mistake. This at first seemed good, and I thought that this was the spirit in which a medical meeting should be conducted. But even here, I realized that something strange was going on. The senior men were all very successful and very secure in themselves. As a result they could well afford to talk of failures. But this in itself seemed to be catching. It became the thing to do. To talk of one's failures became a sign of status in itself because it demonstrated to this type of audience how very secure the speaker was.

I think most of us unconsciously do things for status in one way or another. Then when we realize what has been going on we feel rather ashamed. It was just that the striving for status at the Rio meeting was so blatant and unadorned that it seemed to offend.

Macumba and the Casting out of Devils

I had heard something of macumba, the strange Brazilian cult in which evil spirits are cast out of the body. So as soon as I arrived at the meeting I started to make enquiries about it. Whenever I brought up the subject with one of the local doctors, he would immediately show great interest in telling me about it, but as soon as I asked where I might see some of it, there was always a quick change in the subject of conversation. It was only after considerable persistence on my part that I eventually persuaded a senior doctor from the medical congress to take me to a meeting of macumba. At this stage I really knew nothing at all about it, but I felt secure enough in being taken there by another doctor. I did not know what I was in for.

We drove off late at night to a dingy area on the outskirts of Rio. The meeting was held in a kind of chapel. There was an open area dominated by a huge figure of Christ, and at the side there was a figure of St George. Behind this there were rows of seats. On either side of the open area there stood a line of priests and priestesses. They were all coloured. All were dressed in white, the men wore a garb like white pyjamas and the women were dressed in white cotton gowns.

All were smoking huge cigars. This was incongruous enough in front of the great image of Christ. But worse than this, each person as he came in stood in front of one of these attendants, and was openly hypnotized. This was done by staring into their eyes and making passes in front of them. It was done in exactly the same way as Mesmer hypnotized his patients in Paris in the days before the revolution. When they had been hypnotized, they wandered about rather vacantly in the open area before the image of Christ.

Then the drumming started. It was awful, impelling drumming; primitive, something that went right through you. Still in deep hypnosis they began to dance to it. Gently at first, then the drumming and dancing seemed to take over their bodies and minds completely, and they danced without knowing what they were doing.

Wicked spirits were being driven from the body. It was a terrible experience for these people dancing – dancing like automatons to the irresistible command of the drums. Their bodies were contorted. With each beat of the drums the same bizarre movement would be repeated. An arm would be shot out, the head pulled back, the eyes rolled upwards, the back arched as if it would break. On and on they went, men and women, white and coloured. As I watched, three different men were thrown into fits. I have seen many fits, both epileptic and hysterical, but I have never seen ones of greater violence. As one man lay convulsing on the floor, one of the priests stood over him with one leg on each side of his body. Apparently this was to restain him lest he suffer severe bodily injury. As he stood over him, the priest gradually took on some of the contorted movements of the victim, and I realized that this was part of it. The wicked spirit was leaving the victim, and was coming temporarily to inhabit the body of the priest. As the priest became more contorted, the man on the floor became easier. Then the evil spirit left the priest. He was normal again, and he helped the man on the floor to his feet. All the time the other dancers, deep in their trance, were milling around paying no attention whatsoever to the antics of those around them.

So it went on. Evil spirits were exorcised from the body. And then the rhythm of the drums gradually changed. This was the signal for the good spirits to come and inhabit their bodies. And I am sure that they felt this to be so. Ecstasy must be a very wonderful state which few of us will ever experience. But in Rio I stood beside people who were in ecstasy, and that in itself was sufficient to give me a feeling of awe. Faces that had been mis-shapen as though contorted by evil, gradually changed; and the calm and serenity of a Renaissance madonna came upon them.

Perhaps I should say something of my own feelings. On the way to the meeting my friend explained through an interpreter that he had done some psychological work with people who practice macumba. Although he could speak no English I was reassured by this. But as soon as we arrived, he went up to the chief priestess. From the way they talked together it was clear that they were old friends. Then she made some passes in front of him, and he went momentarily into a trance; and my feeling of security in his company quickly faded. Later he led me up and stood me in front of one of the priestesses who was hynotizing the participants. The old black hag stared steadily into my eyes with half closed lids. She said nothing. She just puffed clouds of foul smoke in my face from her huge cigar. There was the awful rhythm of the drums resounding through every organ of my body. There were all the people milling around me in deep trance. I knew enough of hypnosis to realize what the old hag in front of me was doing. Very slowly and imperceptibly she started to sway with the music. I realized that I was standing in front of an expert in my own field. If I unconsciously started to sway in sympathy with the movement of her body I too would become hypnotized. If this happened, as likely as not, I would develop these bizarre movements or have a convulsion on the floor just like the others. The terrible drumming and the strange behaviour of those deep in hypnosis all around me added to the strain, but I managed to resist her; and after a while she dismissed me.

Finally the drumming stopped; and it was over. But the participants came out of their trance only slowly. Some ten or fifteen minutes after the ceremony had stopped I was able to take three of the participants by the hand, and raise their arm above their head without them being aware of what I was doing. When I let go the hand, in each case the arm remained held in the air. This is catalepsy, a common clinical sign of hypnosis. The interesting point was the persistence of catalepsy for so long after the finish of the ceremony.

So that was macumba. I had seen something which does not

seem to belong to the present-day world. Yet, I am told that some millions of people follow this strange cult, and that it is not confined to the poor, the coloured or the uneducated, and in fact many sophisticated businessmen and professional people are among its members. What does it all mean? Perhaps the best lesson from it is simply that primitive drives still lurk in the mind of civilized man, and given the right circumstances these can be given terrible expression.

We must remember that the participants of macumba regard themselves as Christians and look upon these rites as an expression of their Christian religion. I understand that this view is accepted, perhaps with some misgiving, by the local church authorities.

The origin of the cult is simple enough. The West African slaves that were imported into Brazil brought with them a primitive folklore. With it there came the story of the hero who personified goodness and who killed the serpent which represented evil. When Christian missionaries taught them about St George killing the dragon, they accepted the story as their own legend. With this impetus the worship of St George became widespread in Brazil. It is now an integral part of the macumba cult; while the drumming and the use of trance are a tribal heritage which has become revived in this pseudo-Christian setting.

The Samba in Rio

As with most medical meetings arrangements were made to show visitors local things of interest. There were the usual sight-seeing trips, and one night, as an alternative to the theatre, we were offered a visit to a samba club. I thought that this might show me something of life in Rio, so I set off in a bus with about twenty South American doctors, only one of whom could speak English.

It was a full hour's journey to an outer suburb. We eventually stopped at a large, cheaply constructed hall. There were a few seats around the walls, and the body of the hall was filled with some hundreds of people, milling around and talking in animated fashion. Then the music started, loud music that went all through you, and they started to dance. It was quite new to me. I had seen nothing like it. The rhythm seemed to take over. They danced, not with each other, but with the music. A lad as he danced would come to a girl and they would dance together, the one in front of the other, and then they would move off dancing by themselves with only the music. There were people of all ages, and of all colours through black to white. Many were in a light trance, dancing on their own, utterly abandoned to the rhythm of the music.

In the centre of the floor was one of the strangest sights I have ever seen. It was a group of Negroes, men and women, about a dozen or fifteen in all. They were dressed in pale blue costumes in the style of the court of Louis the Fourteenth. The women wore great crinolines and carried fans. On their heads above the coarse blackness of their Negro faces, they each wore the traditional powdered wig of white curls. The men were dressed to match in light blue knickerbockers, white stockings, buckled shoes, and lace cuffs falling down over their horny black hands. Like the women, the men wore traditional powdered wigs. The group in the centre remained isolated from the others dancing around them. They moved about among themselves, making a poor imitation of courtly gestures, the women with their fans and the men with their lace handkerchiefs. Two of the men had long, silver-topped staffs which they used in pantomime fashion to create an air of grandeur. And when I first saw this, I thought it was a kind of pantomime. And I laughed to myself. Then I realized that it was not a joke. It was no pantomime. They were all deadly serious. It struck me deeply, and I felt desperately sorry for them. Never have I felt so sorry for a coloured person. They were living in a kind of fantasy. They were important. Others were looking at them, envying them their gorgeous clothes, and their white hair. They were great people. Those around could all see it. The fans, the handkerchiefs and the long staffs all showed it.

They stayed in the centre of the hall bestowing patronage on the dancers around them.

Then one of the dancers caught my eye. She was a coloured woman in her middle twenties wearing smart European clothes. She was dancing with utter abandon. She was infected with the rhythm of the music and she herself infected those who came near her. She found herself in the centre of a ring of dancing men and women. They were captivated by her, watching her as they themselves danced to the music. One man came and danced in front of her, and when he did, his dancing changed. It was now all through him. He moved off again. Another came, and so it was with him.

This was the Samba of Brazil, something I had never seen or even imagined. The evening drew on. It was nearly three o'clock. It would be over soon. I was very tired. I wanted to sit down but the chairs were all taken. So I went out to the bus and sat there by myself waiting for it to finish. It was a slum neighbourhood. A mist had come up making yellow haloes around the few street lights. People were beginning to leave the hall in twos and threes. Then I noticed some of the costumed Negroes. They were tired now. The grand manner had gone. They walked past the bus. It had been a great night. They were tired, but happy. Two of them took off their shoes. They turned down the narrow side street lined with slum houses. So tired, so happy, they walked like drunken people reeling into one another. One of the women took off her wig and carried it under her arm. The street light showed up her frizzly hair. She walked on and disappeared in the mist.

The doctors came and filled the bus. They had had a good night. The English-speaking one came and sat beside me. But I found I could not talk to him. It was all too pathetic.

A Modern Yogi

Last year I was to attend an international meeting of psychiatrists in Madrid. A new flight had been opened up from Australia to Johannesburg. So I decided to take it and see something of Africa on the way. The plane refuels at Mauritius so I arranged to stop off there for a few days.

This little island, isolated in the Southern Indian Ocean, is quite an unusual place. It is a British colony, but most of the inhabitants are Indian, and the Europeans speak French. After driving around the island on the usual sight-seeing tour I visited a Hindu temple. When the priest realized that I was genuinely interested, he suggested that I should meet a famous yogi who lived on the island. I spent most of the next day driving from place to place before I was able to find him. But when I did, I was well rewarded.

I have told you something of the various yogis I have met in India, Nepal and Burma. These were all practitioners of Yoga in the classical sense. They were traditionalists. They aimed to practise the art as it had been handed down from teacher to pupil for three thousand years. They were scholarly, but scholarly only as regards the ancient writings of the Hindus. They had a disregard for what is new, and had little knowledge of science or modern psychology.

This yogi was different. He was a modern. He knew both worlds. Besides his native tongue he spoke fluent English. He knew the Hindu classics and also the basis of modern scientific thought. He had meditated in the Himalayan mountains, but had also visited places of Western learning.

When I first met him I did not know all this. He was living in a house on a cliff overlooking the ocean. He talked with me, not so much in the usual way of a yogi, but more as a professional colleague. Quite unlike the traditional yogi, he smiled and laughed, and allowed himself free and easy conversation. This put me on guard. Yogis do not behave like this. I thought this man must be one of the charlatans who adopt the pose of a yogi for their own ends. But as we talked I learned that this was not so. He was not a trickster. Without him explaining it to me, I came to realize that he was a man who was trying to create a synthesis in his own person of what was best of both traditional eastern philosophy and of modern western learning. I was fascinated by the idea. Then the thought came to me with startling clarity that in some kind of groping fashion this was what I myself was trying to do, only from the other side, as it were.

Some of the things about him put me off. They seemed incongruous. I found myself thinking that the ease with which he laughed was out of place in a holy man. Then I realized the extent to which I myself was bound by traditional ideas. The wise man, the holy man, is above all things, natural. Laughter is a more natural response than eastern withdrawal and non-attachment. Then as we talked together on the lawn looking out over the ocean from the cliff-edge, it suddenly seemed that yoga non-attachment was nothing more than a monstrous defence against the individual's own anxiety. As such it made the attainment of yoga peace of mind so very much easier. This man had a real inner calm, but he lacked the deep serenity of the great yogis I had met. Perhaps this is the price of laughter and normal emotional responses.

Then I realized that other factors also came into it. To me it seemed that he was attempting something new. This was an integration of the East with the West in his own person. If it is something new I should not expect it to be complete. This could account for the minor incongruities which I thought I observed.

We talked of serious things of body and mind, of man and God. And what he said gave me great heart. From my experience with hypnosis I had come to some conclusions which were quite contrary to yoga teaching, and at the same time were barely acceptable to the few Western colleagues who are sufficiently interested to discuss such matters. This man, with a background so different from mine, had come to a way of thinking remarkably similar to my own. And it does give you heart just to feel that you are not in complete isolation, and that some other person sees your point of view. This is how I felt as we talked together.

I asked him about meditation and the state of mind of the individual in deep meditation. He spoke of the mind as being in a state of 'unmodified consciousness', and that in deep meditation consciousness was 'primordial'. These ideas of the swami fitted in exactly with my Atavistic Theory of Hypnosis and the relationship of hypnosis to the state of mind in deep meditation. I believe that the basic factor in hypnosis is that the mind goes back, as it were, and functions as it did many thousands of years ago at the very dawn of the human race. In this state, the mind functions with great simplicity. I believe that the same process occurs in deep meditation. Many hypnotists have rejected these ideas in the belief that the state of mind in hypnosis is quite the reverse of what I suggest, that it is, in fact, a supra-normal state of consciousness, not a regressed one. It has always seemed to me that both hypnotists and yogis have a kind of vested interest in the state of mind with which they work, and it is more satisfying for them to think of it as something supra-normal rather than atavistic. During our discussion the swami volunteered that deep meditation was a form of autohypnosis. This had been denied by all the other yogis with whom I had discussed the matter. I told the swami of the intense opposition of some Indians to a paper which I had read suggesting that in yoga meditation the mind functioned in a very simple, primitive fashion. He smiled, and said that three hundred and sixty degrees is the same as zero.

I think that this is a very fundamental observation, at least as far as the mind is concerned. Really great things are very simple. There is an inherent simplicity in true greatness. In fact it is the quality of simplicity which often distinguishes what is great from what is not. This applies to great thoughts, great actions and great things, and more than ever to the mind that begets them.

In this context the swami's comment would seem true of hypnosis and meditation. When the mind is functioning in a simple or 'primordial' fashion it may be capable of great things which are in fact the result of an apparently 'supra-normal' state of consciousness.

I asked what was his way of helping people who came to him. He said he did this by prayer and by making them laugh. He felt that if he could be happy, then they were happy too. This was a very simple exposition of the way in which one person will take on the mood of another.

At the time I was with him, he had an invitation to visit the local hospital, and he asked if I would care to accompany him.

It was an old army barracks converted to medical use, a poor hospital for poor people, where the doctor only visited certain days. The swami had a large bag of boiled sweets. He gave one to each patient, putting a sweet in his hand, and as he did so he enclosed the patient's hand with his own, and muttered a few words. He was smiling and cheerful. Many of the patients were sick and in pain. Their eyes showed that they had little to look forward to other than discomfort, solitude and death. The swami was both calm and happy. This was something quite different from the calm of the other yogis whom I had met. Theirs has always been the calm of detachment. But this man had both calm and warmth. As he pressed their fingers, their expression changed. They gained by his visit. This was quite unlike traditional yoga practice with its mental detachment and unconcern for the suffering for others. I felt that I was witness of something new, something that might open up new horizons in the future.

We were accompanied around the hospital by his followers. These were a small group of young Indians in their late teens and early twenties, both sexes, all very devoted to the swami, and very idealistic in themselves. Among them was a blonde European girl. She had heard of the swami where she lived in South Africa, and had come to Mauritius to study under him. Her attitude to the swami was open adulation. Her big round eyes hardly moved from his face. I gradually pieced together some of the story. Several times she had booked her return flight. But on each occasion she had cancelled it in order to stay just a little longer with the swami. She was finally flying back to South Africa the next day, on the same plane as myself. At any mention of this, her big eyes noticeably filled. But there was to be no hold-up this time. The swami himself had arranged for a friend to pick him up in the early hours of the morning and drive him and the girl to the airport on the other side of the island. Next morning as I was being driven there myself in the dark before dawn I wondered if she would make it this time. They arrived all right, the swami calm and smiling with an occasional laugh, and the blonde white girl holding back her tears. Then not to be out of it, his youthful followers scrambled out of an old car ostensibly to say good-bye to the girl; but their interest was clearly in the man and not in the blonde.

As I sat in the plane I tried to evaluate what I had seen of the swami. It seemed beyond all doubt that he was a gifted person. I began to think how the mind of man has developed. Over countless generations we have evolved our way of logical thought, and on the humanistic side for the most part we have progressed beyond barbarism and savagery. We must assume that the human mind is developing still further. If this be so, where do we look for those who are in the forefront of this great evolutionary venture? If it is intellectual capacity that is our main concern, then we should name the Nobel Prize winners. But to my knowledge at least some of these are not well balanced men. Perhaps we should consider those who display the greatest drive for humanity as the most advanced of men. But several reports have shown that many members of the peace corps and human rights organizations are largely activated by neurotic motivations. Perhaps the person at the forefront of human development is neither the intellectual nor the humanist as we ordinarily know them, but rather someone such as the swami, who has achieved an integration of his own personality, and can lead others to do likewise.

11 SOUTH AFRICA

The Symbolic Painting of the Mentally Disturbed

I flew on from Mauritius to Johannesburg. Here I had been invited to give three lectures on the same day, each on quite different subjects and in different localities. The first lecture was held in a mental hospital of truly magnificent appointments. But this was for Europeans only; mentally ill coloured folk are treated in very different surroundings. The lecture concerned some work which I have done in helping mentally disturbed persons by getting them to paint. In fact the main purpose of my trip was to attend a meeting of psychiatrists in Madrid where some of my paintings were to be exhibited. It is a strange thing, but many schizophrenic patients will paint quite readily if they are given painting materials, although they have never painted anything before in their lives. It seems that the schizophrenic illness does away with one's normal inhibitions. As a result of this all manner of ideas which have been disturbing the patient are on the threshold of expression. In these circumstances, if the patient be given brush and paint he will express the ideas which have been troubling him in what he paints. It often happens that he will express ideas in this way which he is unable to express in words. This comes about by use of symbolism. By this means he may come to express complicated ideas concerning the basic problems of life, such as birth and death, problems of sexuality and homosexuality, and the very purpose of life. These symbolic paintings of the schizophrenic patient are very similar to the surrealistic pictures of some modern artists. An extraordinary aspect of these paintings is that the disturbed patient is commonly quite unaware of the meaning of the symbolism of the picture which he has painted. Very often the meaning only becomes clear to both the patient and doctor after the patient has been brought to talk about the painting both as a whole and in its individual elements. In this way I have been able to help some patients back to health by giving them understanding of the conflicts deep within their minds which had brought about their illness.

An interesting feature is that many patients while they are mentally ill paint symbolic pictures of great strength and meaning; but when they recover from their illness they are either unable to paint at all or simply paint pictures of the chocolate-box variety which lack any character or meaning at all. The reason for this is that the inhibitory processes of the patient's mind are restored as he recovers his normal health, and these basic conflicts no longer find easy expression. This has happened with several patients whom I have treated. One of these patients had two or three relapses in the course of her illness. Each time she relapsed she became quite mad, but at the same time she was able to paint pictures of first class quality; but when she was well again, she painted only rubbish.

This was the subject of my lecture, and I was flattered to find from subsequent questions that a number of those in the audience had read a book which I once wrote describing some of this work.

It is easy to feel flattered. I remember being disappointed with myself that I should feel this way. Somehow it seemed a rather cheap emotion. But on thinking about it now, I wonder why I was so ashamed of my inner feelings. Perhaps I was harking back to childhood teaching that one should not be too pleased with success, or perhaps the disregard of the yogis concerning such matters was still fresh in my mind. It just seems that a feeling of pleasure is the normal reaction to success. In this way it would seem that both yoga, and the traditional teaching of our schools, err in trying to suppress our normal emotional responses.

An African Township

The next day I was taken to see an African township on the outskirts of Johannesburg. I had previously written to a psychiatrist friend asking if he could show me something of the way in which the Africans lived. I had not realized that under the apartheid laws Africans are not permitted to live in the city itself. They work there, but they are not allowed to live within the city limits. Instead they are segregated into townships outside the city, and come in to work each day by train. This segregation of the races works in both directions. Europeans are not allowed to enter the townships. My friend told me of the difficulties he had had in arranging the visit. He had to explain that I was a visiting psychiatrist interested in human behaviour but with no interest in politics. After all these difficulties we were in fact taken around in very friendly fashion by the government official, who is responsible for the administration of the townships. I thought it interesting that neither my friend nor the two other doctors who went with us had ever been in an African township before, although they had lived in Johannesburg all their lives.

There is poverty here; but it is not the poverty of utter lack of food and physical need that one sees in India. The people of the townships all appeared well nourished; and they all have their houses. They are small houses, but provide the bare necessities. There is water, and the houses are sewered, but the toilets have to be flushed manually with a bucket of water. There is no real overcrowding as an African is not allowed to come to live in the township unless there is a vacancy for him. In the material sense they were just above the level of real poverty. But there is a poverty of outlook which must surely starve the spirit. Row upon row of the same miserable little houses. Children playing in the gutters of the unmade streets. We think of suburbia in our own cities; but this was a nightmare suburbia, with all the sameness and drabness only a hundred times worse.

Having been told it was rare for Europeans to visit the townships, I went there expecting that we would be subject to hostile gestures from the Africans in the streets. But this was far from the case. Men stopped and nodded as we drove past. Girls waved, baring their white teeth in broad smiles. I wondered why they were not resentful. Surely they should be. It seems that the African when left to himself is an easygoing fellow who rarely bears resentment. It is we who have taught him to feel that way; and you can see it so clearly in his kinsfolk in Harlem.

But however well the townships may be administered, and whatever precautions are taken against overcrowding, they still remain places of destitution. It is always the same. The urban community, which is materially better off, is more destitute than a rural community on a near subsistence level. The large playgrounds and the bleak community halls of the newer townships only show the emptiness of it all. The administrative officer showed me with pride a newly constructed beer garden where the inhabitants could sit and drink amid tinsel and all that is tawdry. The poverty-stricken people of a rural community with earth floor huts and the village well live better than this. They may be destitute, but they are not tawdry. They follow the plough, plant the seed and reap the crop. They must surely sense that they are part of a great rhythm of things. There is still some kind of human dignity in an impoverished rural existence, which playgrounds and beer halls could not possibly give to the African townships.

The same segregation applies to the few wealthy Africans. Some had been permitted to build quite large houses on the fringe of the township. These Africans have their cars and their servants just as their white masters.

I was taken to the local medicine shop. It was a new building such as might be seen in the shopping areas of any American town. There were the usual glass show-cases. These were full of the stock-in-trade of traditional African medicine. There were dried bats and lizards, and powdered herbs and strange-shaped roots. And suspended from the ceiling, hovering over me like a beast of prey was a huge dead bird with out-stretched wings. But the traditional merged with the modern. Outside the shop was the owner's new car, its gaudy colours signifying to all the status of the driver. But what seemed strangest to me was that this shop catered for sophisticated urban Africans, who worked each day in the great city of Johannesburg. Most of these people would claim to be completely Westernized. But when sickness comes it is different. The veneer of civilization is shed like a coat, and the African returns to the ways of his forebears. But the African is not alone in this. Sickness with its pain and the threat of death affects us all alike. We drop the façade of our way of life. And with this goes another process. In sickness we regress a little. We tend to revert to childish patterns of behaviour and a more primitive way of looking at things. There is often a desire to be treated as a little boy or little girl, and of course being in bed emphasizes this. As a part of the regression, I have often noticed how patients under the stress of serious illness revert to the beliefs of childhood. This includes religious belief. Many people who change their religion in later adolescence, may live their whole life in their new belief, only to forsake it again in the regression of serious illness. So it is with the African. He is a civilized man until overtaken by the stress of illness. Then he regresses a little, and reverts to the ancestral ways of his tribe.

We returned to my friend's home. It was good to leave the squalor of the township behind, and get back to the comfort of his elegant home. I noticed the elaborate burglar alarm system on the doors and windows. Later I asked about it and was told that every house is protected in this way, downstairs and upstairs as well. It is not safe even to post a letter after dark. This is the way they live.

But the white folk of South Africa and Rhodesia live well. It is a way of life for which they have fought, and which they are not readily going to abandon. With servants they are freed from most of the material chores of domestic living. With so much more time there would seem endless opportunities for a fuller and better life. But it does not always work out quite like this. There is elegance and gracious living, and time for leisure, particularly for the women. But with many it does not lead to the fuller life that one might expect. In fact there is often only a greater emptiness comparable only with the new beer garden in the township with its tinsel and all the tawdry trappings with which it was adorned.

I expect that relief from the tedium of the basic tasks of life, the gathering and preparation of food, is one of the primary aims of civilization. With it goes the assumption that man is thus freed for better things, although it still remains uncertain just what those better things really are. Here in South Africa and Rhodesia there is a group of people who are in fact freed from many basic chores, but I was unable to see that there was any significant move towards those better things, whatever they might be.

A Strange Animal

I was now ready to start on the project which had brought me to Africa. This was to try to find some witch-doctors, and see if their practices could throw any light on some of the lesser known states of mind or reveal anything which might possibly be of use in western medicine for the treatment of nervous illness. I had had a good deal of contact with yogis, Buddhist priests and Zen masters, but I quickly learned that this experience was of little help to me with African witch-doctors. These others, in their own way, are reputable in the eyes of the white man. Europeans at least know where they are, and can show you where to find them. But with witch-doctors it is different. At Salisbury I engaged the manager of the hotel in conversation. Then, when I thought we were getting on well together, I casually asked him where I might find a witch-doctor, as I would be interested to meet such a man. His attitude changed completely.

'There aren't any witch-doctors now.' And he looked at me as if I were a schoolgirl who had been reading imaginative fiction and had thought it real.

I tried out three or four other Europeans around the hotel and in tourist agencies. Each time I was met with the same kind of answer. I began to think that I had failed before I had even got started. Then I hit upon another idea. I hired a car with an African driver who could speak English. I allowed him to drive me about, and show me the usual tourist sights. We engaged in casual conversation; then after about forty minutes of being shown things which I had little interest to see, I brought up the subject of witch-doctors.

'Of course, there are a lot of witch-doctors about, I can take you to a very good one. I go to him myself.'

With this approach I never failed to find witch-doctors in Rhodesia and Kenya. I never missed once. Yet on many occasions I asked Europeans, and they always gave me the same reply.

'Really, there are no witch-doctors here any more.'

I later came to realize that this was just an example of the way in which the European colonist isolates himself from the native life that is going on all around him. Of course it was the same with the British in India. They provided law and order with justice and administrative efficiency, but they isolated themselves from the people, not only socially but intellectually as well, so that Hinduism and Yoga were looked upon as nothing but pagan practices. But that was a generation ago, and since that time greater understanding has come between the East and West, and the Native and the European. But here in Africa the same situation still continues. This isolation of the European from the Africans with the consequent lack of understanding of what is in the other fellow's mind, would seem to me to be one of the major difficulties in finding a reasonable solution for the present political problems.

Everywhere I went there was evidence of this lack of knowledge and understanding of the Africans. While having dinner on a farm, I heard the beating of drums. It was explained to me that the workmen and their families lived on the farm, and on Saturday night they had a party with drinking and dancing, and that this often continued all night and all the next day. But nobody seemed to know what it was really all about. The next afternoon the drums were still sounding so I asked if I could see what was going on.

They were dancing in the dirt between the huts. Men, women and girls were all half drunk or more so. After the initial shock of our visit they were quite open in their friendliness. There was no sign of hostility at our intrusion. The African is in fact a simple and friendly person. Gestures were made inviting me to have a drink. This was a fermented maize beverage which looked like thin gruel. By gestures I asked them to continue dancing. They did so and the drums struck up with renewed gusto. They danced, churning up the dust as they did so, and covering the rags they were wearing with dirt and grime. The drummers brought out the rhythm, banging the hide of the drums with their bare hands. Children of all ages gathered round, black skins, dust covered faces, running noses and shining white teeth. Half drunk women with babies danced with the child strapped to their backs. The more they danced, the more the dust went everywhere and the more they drank.

They were flattered by our interest, and a discussion arose which obviously concerned ourselves. Then with much good humour we were ushered to a little clearing a short distance from the huts. It was indicated that we should sit on a log and wait. The drummers came and sat down, while the men formed a group on one side and the women on the other. There were broad smiles all around, and a general air of expectancy. Then the drummers started, and the two groups of men and women clapped in time with their hands. Then a man rushed into the centre of the area, and started to dance about at great speed. The whole of his body, his face, and his head were covered with feathers, so that it was impossible to see his features. His arms and legs were bare. As he danced he kept kicking up the dried earth in clouds of dust all over himself and anyone nearby. Sometimes he fell on the ground, still kicking his feet in the earth, and scooping up the dirt in his hands and throwing it over his body. The native onlookers were all smiles and white teeth as they watched the performance, and kept clapping and singing with the drums. I gathered that the dancer was imitating a cock or a hen, but I was not able to confirm this. He eventually ran off into the tall dry grass which surrounded the little arena.

Thinking the show was over, we made a move to return to the homestead. But with many gestures we were restrained to wait where we were. The African spectators were obviously expecting something to happen. They kept scanning the long grass which surrounded us. I thought they were watching for the dancer to return. But no. There was great excitement, and the self-appointed master-of-ceremonies rushed over to us pointing into the long grass. Twenty or thirty yards away, partially hidden in the grass, I could see a strange beast made of straw. It was like a huge bird, but with the head of a ram. I immediately started in its direction so as to see it more clearly. But I was promptly stopped by the master-of-ceremonies holding up his hands and shaking his head violently. So I stood there and watched as best I could as it moved about and bobbed up and down. I think there were two men in it. But I could not see it clearly although it was quite close. It was frustrating in the extreme. But this of course was part of the mystique. If I had been able to see it clearly, it would probably have appeared as a rather laughable childish contraption. But as it was, it was a thing of mystery. I do not

know its meaning, and whether or not it aimed to represent
some totem animal of tribal significance.

We returned to the homestead only a few hundred yards distant. The owner of the farm had lived there all his life, but he
could tell me nothing of the strange happenings which occurred on his property. This is what I mean when I say that the
European seems to be quite out of touch with the African and
quite oblivious as to what goes on in his mind.

Chased by an Elephant

I flew from Salisbury to Livingstone to see the Victoria Falls.
The plane called at Kariba, and circled low so that all could
see the great dam where the Zambesi lies in a narrow gorge between two mountains. Then on to Livingstone. But there were
problems here. The airport is on one side of the river in
Zambia, and the hotel is across the bridge in Southern
Rhodesia. There were customs formalities on both sides. Then
it all had to be repeated again because the best view of the
falls is from the Zambian side; then back again to the hotel
with two more visits to the customs. But it was worth it. The
falls must surely be one of the grandest sights of nature. No
wonder that they were regarded with awe and mystery by the
native Africans.

I too was moved by the sight of the falls. I expect it is a
common human characteristic to be moved by spectacles of
natural grandeur, such as vistas of the Alps or the Himalayas, or even the view from an aeroplane window. It brings
a feeling of wonder and awe. And with awe comes a realization of the mystery of life and an inner awareness of some
guiding principle. So it is with us. So it was for generations of
Africans who worshipped their gods and evoked their spirits
in the mist of the falls. But why should such feelings come
to us only when we are confronted with nature in her ex-
travagant moods. After all, the great falls at Livingstone are
a relatively simple matter. We are familiar with the laws that
govern the flow of water. Man himself has made waterfalls by
damming rivers in the mountains. There is more wonder in
the growth of a blade of grass. And I realized that I was like
the primitive African seeing wonder in things only when they
are presented on a grand scale.

That evening I hired a car and driver to see the national park along the bank of the Zambesi. The driver was anxious to show me some hippos, and we stopped at a parking bay beside the river. It was still and calm. Here, above the falls, the Zambesi is very wide and flows quietly and peacefully as if unaware of the terrible plunge it is soon to make into the gorge. The driver wandered off to see what he could see, and I was left with my thoughts. Then I noticed the huge footprints of an elephant just beside me. Without thinking of possible consequences I started to follow the footprints. I was obviously hot on his trail as there were fresh droppings still wetting the sand. Then the thought suddenly came to me, 'What do I do if I meet the elephant?' My enthusiasm promptly left me, and I returned to the car. We drove on. It was now dusk. Then some twenty or thirty yards from the track there was an elephant with two baby elephants, and a little farther distant there was a huge bull elephant. I made the driver stop so that we could watch them. The mother elephant was feeding, bundling sheaves of the long dry grass into her mouth. We watched. Then suddenly she put up her ears and rushed towards us. The driver panicked, revved the car like mad, and we shot off as if a hundred devils were after us. The elephant ran along the road a little way; then stopped and wandered off into the scrub with her two little ones. The driver was in a real state of fear, but I managed to get him to stop. We waited a few minutes while he calmed down, and I eventually persuaded him to back cautiously down the track to see if the bull elephant was still there. He was; and then I understood why the mother, and not the father, had chased us. He was busy skirmishing with a huge black shape. I could not see it sufficiently clearly to be sure whether it was a hippo or a rhino. We watched for a while in the dusk and then drove off.

The part of this little incident which remains most vivid in my mind is the terrifying appearance of the elephant when it put up its huge ears. All over the world one sees tourist posters of a great benign elephant looking down peacefully on a car load of tourists. My advice is, 'Don't believe it.'

Throwing the Bones

On the way back from the Victoria Falls there was a delay of some three or four hours at Bulawayo where I had to change planes. So I hired a car, and after some casual talk with the driver, I asked about witch-doctors. He was only too pleased to take me to the witch-doctor that he himself attended.

He lived, of course, in the township, or African quarter, just outside the main town. His house was larger than the others, and the car outside was further evidence of his prosperity.

I always contrived to meet a witch-doctor as an equal. In order to be sure that such people would never have the feeling that I was just a tourist who wanted to take photos of them, I purposely did not carry a camera. Instead I always went out of my way to treat a witch-doctor with respect. I would send the driver to speak to him first, and to explain that I was a visiting doctor who worked in much the same way as he did, and that I would be grateful if I could talk with him. This approach must have appealed to them as each time they welcomed me in friendly fashion, talked openly, and disclosed their arts without reserve. There was only one exception to this. The incident happened in Uganda, when a witch-doctor thought that I was an agent of the government who had come to persecute him.

At first the man in Bulawayo was rather taken aback by my visit, but as soon as he recovered from his surprise he was open and friendly. He was a man of about thirty-five, tall, lithe, good looking and well dressed in European clothes. I was soon to learn that there are really two types of witch-doctors. There are the urban ones, who work in the African townships on the outskirts of the cities, and the rural ones who live in the villages. The urban ones, like this man, are westernized, live in good houses, and carry on their business in very much the same way as our suburban doctors.

I was struck by his appearance and bearing. He was a man who was obviously well above average as a person. He had something about him which put him apart from the ruck of African humanity. In fact this goes for the witch-doctors in general. They are rather superior people. One feels that they are better integrated in their personality than the average African. They are, in fact, people whom one might expect to be leaders; and of course, they are in their way, as the witch-doctor has status, and in virtue of this exerts a powerful influence on those around him.

Just as in the case of psychiatrists, different witch-doctors work in different ways. And, just like psychiatrists, each witch-doctor usually sticks to his favourite method of treatment, but on occasion may dabble in one of the other methods. Some work with trance, some with prayer, some with magic and some throw the bones.

My friend at Bulawayo threw the bones. This is probably the most common technique of witch-doctors, and there are several variations in the art. The bones consist of a number of small pieces each about an inch long. This man told me that his were bits of hippopotamus and crocodile bones. They are usually very worn from being continually handled, and it is difficult to know exactly what they might be, but once or twice with different witch-doctors I thought I recognised fragments of human bones.

When throwing the bones the witch-doctor sits on the ground with his legs wide apart in front of him. He then takes the bones, usually six in number, in his cupped hands, and shakes them violently as one might shake dice. He then casts the bones on the ground. Typically, he looks at them for a moment, then gathers them up again and repeats the process. This may be repeated many times. By the way in which the bones fall he is able to interpret the wish of the spirits and the workings of magic. And of course, the actual bones develop some ill-defined magic qualities in themselves.

Throwing the bones is a very important part of the witch-doctor's magic. But the idea that the gods may reveal their will in matters of chance is common in many cultures. Throughout the East, in temples and in shrines, one may find sets of curved wooden blocks. After prayer and making an offering, the pilgrim takes the blocks in his hands and throws them on the ground. In this way he determines the pleasure of the gods, and ascertains whether or not the time is propitious for some venture which he is about to undertake.

There is in fact a deep-rooted, but unconscious idea within all of us that the chance fall of inert things can somehow be influenced by magic or even by our own mind. This principle is well illustrated by the way in which the golfer sways his body after he has made a long putt in an unconscious attempt to guide the ball as it rolls towards the hole. The sway of the body works by sympathetic magic on the course of the ball. The unconscious nature of the whole process is shown by the way that we only do it when we are completely preoccupied

E

about the ball, and are in fact quite unaware that we are moving our body at all. It is the delight of press photographers to catch golfers and bowlers in such attitudes.

This is one of the strange ways in which our mind works. But even more strangely, parapsychologists, those scientists who work in this area, have shown that sometimes the fall of dice seem to have been influenced to a statistically significant degree by mental concentration. This is technically known as psychokinesis.

It is very hard to obtain any clear idea just how the witch-doctor interprets the fall of the bones. I very much doubt if there are any standard rules. It seemed to me that each witch-doctor made his own interpretations according to his feeling at the moment. Some of them become very preoccupied when throwing the bones, and would appear to be in a light trance, but this is not always the case. Some speak of hearing hallucinatory voices of spirits or angels, but I do not know how common this might be. The end result of throwing the bones is that the witch-doctor gives the patient some advice on how to rid himself of his bewitchment. This may be a matter of taking herbal medicines or performing some magic ritual.

To the African, anything which does not have some obvious cause is due to bewitchment. Thus illness is due to bewitchment, but a broken leg is not. The failure of a woman to bear children is due to bewitchment, and is a common complaint about which the witch-doctor is consulted. But his practice extends far beyond personal illness. A failure of the crop, the infertility of a cow, a wife's bad temper may all be due to bewitchment; and the witch-doctor is naturally the proper person to consult on such matters.

Any failure of a man's sexual potency is due to bewitchment and the help of a witch-doctor is urgently sought. This seems to be quite a common situation. It is interesting, as men are exceedingly sensitive and suggestible about their sexual power. I have actually treated several well educated Australians, who in a strange kind of way had been bewitched although they did not look at it in this light. Each had had a minor sexual failure due to some incidental cause such as over fatigue, low grade influenza or too much alcohol. In each case the woman had derided the man and had humiliated him for his lack of masculinity. In each case this bewitchment had been sufficiently powerful to play upon the man's suggestibility to the extent that his confidence had been destroyed, so that he eventually came to me for psychiatric help. In these cases this is easily given. The psychiatrist helps the patient in very much the same way as the witch-doctor does, by restoring the man's confidence. As with the witch-doctors this may be done either through hypnosis or by suggestion.

I asked the man in Bulawayo how he would proceed in a case of a woman's infertility. For this, the woman must drink a potion which he prescribes, and she must sleep with a spear near her. This was interesting as the spear is the classical phallic symbol of Freudian psychopathology, and women patients of mine, who have been rather starved of sex, have often recounted to me dreams about spears. I gathered that the medicine or potion which he prescribes is not intended to have any physiological effect on the organs concerned, but is rather intended to relieve the woman of the effect of her bewitchment.

I asked if women ever sought his advice on how to avoid becoming pregnant. He said that women sometimes sought advice about this, and his method of helping them was to instruct them to keep a piece of string tied tightly around their waist. If they did this, it would be unlikely that they would become pregnant. From talking with him it was obvious that, if in fact a woman did become pregnant while wearing the string, it would be due to some malevolent bewitchment which had worked against the good magic of the witch-doctor.

This was magic in its simplest form. But the point of greatest interest was that this was a sophisticated African, educated, well-dressed, with his own car; yet apparently in all faith he resorts to magic of the most primitive kind.

There are other fascinating aspects to witch-doctoring. When he is in good health, the African of the cities knows quite well that illness is due to natural causes. But when he is sick, this new-found knowledge tends to desert him; the old ancestral teaching comes to light again, and he knows that he has been bewitched.

I Treat a Witch-Doctor's Wife

Again, in Salisbury I asked my driver if he could take me to a witch-doctor. He knew of a very good one, who was reputed to be a leader in his profession. This was explained to me in just the same way as one might recommend a friend to one's own doctor. He was a big, broad-shouldered, deep-chested, middle aged man, who spoke quite good English. The house was larger than the others in the street, but was old and dirty, and litter covered the floor. Sitting uncertainly on a half broken chair I told him that I too was a doctor like himself. He then explained that he was president of what must be the witch-doctors' association of Rhodesia. To prove his point he produced a blank membership form, all decorated with drawings of the traditional articles of magic. It all seemed so familiar, but so different. We talked, and got on well together. Then he told me he was sorry that he was unable to show me anything as his wife was sick. He then explained that he worked with his wife who would go into a trance and the spirits would tell her what was wrong with the patient. Without her he could do nothing. As we talked on, I had the feeling that I was gaining real rapport with the witch-doctor. So I brought up the subject of his wife's illness again, and asked what was wrong with her. He answered.

'She has terrible pains in the legs.'

Now, pains in the legs, even if they were terrible, did not seem too much of a medical problem to me. So I took a chance.

'If you wish, I shall treat your wife.'

The sudden and enthusiastic way in which he accepted my offer quite frightened me. The wife was brought in. And then I started on a run of extreme good luck. The poor woman looked terribly miserable, and rubbed her legs with her hands. I could see that she was feverish. Then with the witch-doctor acting as interpreter, she explained her throat was sore too. In fact she had an acute tonsillitis, with the pains in the legs which so often go with the condition. My good luck continued. I remembered that I had two aspirin tablets which had been lying at the bottom of my wallet for months. I produced these. Then with the most impressive witch-doctor manner that I could muster, I had her swallow the tablets; and I explained through her husband that in a short while her pains would be gone. As I said this, I went through a ritual of gestures with my hands to psychologically reinforce the effect of the aspirin.

I resumed my conversation with the witch-doctor while the patient sat nearby. In ten minutes she was miraculously improved. The treatment had worked just as I had predicted

In a rather childish way the witch-doctor was extremely impressed. He bubbled over with enthusiasm and good humour. From being perhaps a little dull and apathetic, he became quite wildly excited. In this elated state of mind he insisted that he take me out to meet his witch-doctor friends.

One man was actually treating a patient, but the enthusiasm of my friend was such that we just burst in upon him. The scene was a fairy story reproduction of a witch-doctor at work. The room was very dark and very small, about eight feet by six. The patient sat on a little bench suckling a baby. The witch-doctor sat on the floor with his legs apart throwing the bones. As I looked about me in the murk I could see leopard skins hanging on the wall. There were dead birds on a shelf covered with dust and dirt. There was a half mummified bat, and roots which had grown into strange shapes like mandrakes. Then I noticed stretched across the ceiling just above my head was the skin of a python. If the room were photographed for the scene of a horror film, the critics would be unanimous in saying that it was over-done, and that nothing in reality could ever look like this.

The two witch-doctors started an animated conversation, with my friend obviously telling the other of my success with his wife. Then they seemed to be discussing the patient, who remained quite unconcerned by all this. The witch-doctor then resumed throwing the bones, and each time made various nods and gestures in my direction. These were accompanied by a knowing smile, just as a physician who looks at an x-ray film might smile as he passes it to a colleague in front of the patient. It was clear that he was indicating to me that both he and I knew what was wrong with the patient from the fall of the bones. The two witch-doctors were obviously including me in the treatment of the patient. Then there was a pause and more talk. It was explained to me that it had been discovered that the poor woman was bewitched; and that she had been bewitched by her nephew because he was envious of her kettles. Apparently this had come out in some exploratory history-taking just as one might expect in modern psychiatry. Then it had been confirmed by the bone throwing. The patient was given appropriate medication. But she could not take it just yet as the moon was not in the right phase. She left very happy. The two witch-doctors were very happy; and I was happy too.

13 KENYA

Blood and Milk for Breakfast

Kenya is a wonderful place. There are no colour bars here.
This is an African state ruled by Africans. It is all so different
from South Africa and Rhodesia. Nairobi is a hive of activity where all races bustle about together, European, African
and Indian. I had not realized that there were so many
Indians in East Africa. The hotel had obviously seen better
times, but it was a most interesting place. There were little
tables on a patio opening on to the street. I liked to sit here
and watch the come and go of it all. There was the excitement
of parties leaving on safari. There would be women and girls
in jackets and trousers tailored for the occasion with their
huge gun cases and great cameras. I always marvelled at the
way the departing Land-Rovers were piled high with tents and
bedding, with tins of petrol and water and smiling African
servants. Others would be returning, the occupants, dirty and
stiff, would clamber out, shouting to their friends how many
they had bagged, while the concierge and his assistants un-
packed the precious relics.

When one is by oneself in a crowded place it is impossible
not to overhear snatches of conversation. There was only one
topic among the European tourists. How many lions had they
seen, how many elephants, how many rhinos; how many
this and that of all the lesser breeds of the animal world. In
these circumstances people become expansive and talk to
strangers. I would be brought into conversations. But I was
always a flop. I had to admit that I had not been to any of the
big game reserves, and that my interest was in people rather
than in animals. This was sacrilege. I would try to explain
the error of my ways by telling them that many of the people
in these parts were as interesting as the animals. But no one
listened to me. I was always the odd man out.

There is a strange side issue to the controversy as to whether
we should accord priority to man or beasts. Much of the
wealth of these countries depends on foreign tourists who

come to see the big game. It is obviously in the interest of the country to preserve the game in large numbers. But there is conflict here. Native Africans live from the same pasture as the animals. This applies particularly to the Masai who are nomadic herdsmen. They are proud and unruly, and tend to believe that they have the right to graze their herds where they like. They continually encroach upon the game reserves, where their cattle denude the area at the expense of the native game. Several times I heard the subject hotly debated. Should the pastures be kept for men or animals?

The Masai are interesting people in many ways, but particularly so in the way they have solved the cooking problem which is such a burden to so many of us. They simply live on a diet of blood and milk. With the spear which they habitually carry they snick a vein in the neck of one of their herd, and collect the blood in a gourd. Then they stop the blood flow by plugging the bleeding point with moist clay. They mix the blood with milk and drink it. This is their staple diet.

They are tall, lithe people. The women have the same athletic figure as the men, and they do not seem to run to fat in the same way as most African women do, with their broad shoulders, big breasts, fat bellies and prominent behinds. Both men and women of the Masai wear huge ear-rings. These are suspended from holes in the lobes and in the upper part of the ear. Owing to the weight of the ornaments the ears become stretched, so that it is not uncommon to see people, both men and women, with their ear lobes pulled out of shape to such an extent that they hang down below the level of the collar bone.

Prayers to God in the Sky

I was anxious to see some of the tribal witch-doctors as distinct from those who lived in the towns. My driver had heard of one near Ngong, so we set out to see if we could find him. We stopped near the market place, and the driver left me in the car while he went off to try to find out where the witch-doctor lived.

While he was gone, four or five Masai wandered up to the car. At first I was quite frightened by their huge spears and wild appearance. But they were only curious. One of them noticed the rear-view mirror on the mud-guard. He was absolutely intrigued by his reflection, and he went through all the antics of a child holding his head first on one side and then on the other. I think it must have been the first time he had ever seen his reflection in a mirror. This continued until the driver returned. I must admit that I was glad to see him, as I was certainly not very comfortable with these strange men and their spears.

The witch-doctor lived in a distant village. We drove down endless tracks, but always ended in the wrong place. It was a beautiful day, and I enjoyed every minute of it. Eventually we found him; and we talked with him on a grassy bank outside his hut. He was a big man, calm and strong. There was quite a presence about him. His face was unlined, and there was depth in his eyes. With the driver acting as interpreter I asked him how he treated his patients. Pointing upwards, he said that he prayed to God in the sky. He explained that he would take a lamb or a kid and kill it. Then he would drop the fat in the fire, and the smoke would take his prayer up to God in the sky.

This was said in the calm of utter conviction. I was deeply touched. Here was the simplicity of a child, and strength of an Old Testament prophet. His sincerity was written all over him. From this brief contact, I at once knew that he could cure people, or with the help of God in the sky he could at least make them feel better. And I tried to analyse what made me so sure of all this. It was his personality, of course; just as it is the personality of the doctor, or psychiatrist, that counts. But it is more than this. It is the man himself. And this man was a superior man, calm, well integrated and understanding. It was easy to see how lesser people would lose their anxiety from personal contact with him, and they would feel better as the smoke took his prayers for them up to God in the sky. As we stood there in the clear African sunshine, looking down a wide valley to the blue hills in the distance, I too felt some of his calm.

I asked him more; and he said that he sometimes mixed milk and honey in a gourd, and poured it on the ground. This was an offering which would bring God in the sky to help his patient. I felt the strength of his conviction as he spoke.

I rather wish that I had been content with what I had seen

and heard, for I felt that I had been taken back three or four thousand years to the time when man was first able to conceive the idea of one great god. But I was not content, and I asked for more.

'Are there any other ways you can help your patients?'

Then came the disillusionment. 'Sometimes I pour beer over the patient.'

But of course I should not have felt disillusioned. This was said with the same simple sincerity as he described his prayers to God in the sky. Somehow the idea of pouring the libation of milk and honey from a gourd had been acceptable to me, whereas pouring beer from a can over the patient only seemed ridiculous. But I should not have thought like this. Beer is something which is highly valued by such people, and in these circumstances I am sure that to pour beer is just as significant a libation as is the more traditional milk and honey.

As we drove back, I could not keep thoughts of the man out of my mind. I knew that he had influenced me in the same way as he influenced the Africans who come to him. And I knew that I had gained by the experience.

Witch-Doctor or Witch?

The next day I saw a woman witch-doctor. On this occasion I had another driver. He himself had consulted her about personal problems. She lived in a Kikuyu village, about an hour's drive from Nairobi. We found her hut, and the driver went in to explain my visit; then I was brought into the hut to see her. I had to bend low to fit through the entrance of the dark, round hut. Almost all Africans build their huts round rather than square. The reason for this is simple enough. Everyone knows that spooks collect in corners. In a round hut there are no corners to attract spooks. Only a very foolish person would live in a square hut.

She was a woman of about forty, slender for an African, wild-eyed and rather unpredictable in her movements. She was seated on a stool, and there were five men gathered around her in a semi-circle. It seemed very dark inside the hut, and at first I could not quite make out what was going on. Then I realized that the men were her patients. It was a kind of group treatment, somewhat after the style of that which has become a popular vogue in modern psychiatry at the present time.

The woman witch-doctor welcomed my driver as an old friend. After some rummaging around a stool was found for me, and I was better able to assess things. The woman herself was very much in charge. She spoke loudly and quickly, and laughed in a strange way. She was not a calm person like some of the other witch-doctors. She was dynamic. She tossed her head about as she spoke and jangled her ear-rings. These were of copper and had so stretched her ears that the holes in the lobes were some three or four inches in diameter leaving only a thin rim of flesh. It seemed that she did not quite know what to do with me, so she maintained an animated conversation with my driver and, as is the custom with most witch-doctors, she kept sniffing snuff which she carried in a vessel made from a cow's horn.

She then tried to bring me into the discussion, but the driver was a poor interpreter. It appeared that she used a mixture of herbal medicines, magic and prayer. She was friendly to me because of my driver, but I do not know how honest she was. The time came for me to go. I put some money in her hand. She seemed pleased, and quickly took the money. Then she spat on my hand. I am rather proud of myself in being able to say that I did not react to this; but as soon as we had left I asked the driver why she had spat on me. He was surprised at my asking the question, and explained that this was just an act of friendliness.

Somehow it seemed to me that perhaps she was more witch than witch-doctor. I wonder what gave her this strange power over men. When I first saw her, I thought she may have been schizophrenic. In the middle ages many schizophrenic women, who heard the hallucinatory voice of God or the devil, were burnt as witches. She had the strange appearance of many of those who suffer from this disorder of the mind. Her loud and rather inappropriate laugh, and her quick impulsive movements would be consistent with this condition. I do not know if she heard hallucinatory voices or not. But there are other disorders of the personality besides schizophrenia which have led women to be regarded as witches. Sometimes men fear the sexuality of certain women. This is because of man's innate horror of castration. In Europe during the middle ages, witch-craft was often associated with prostitution. At the inquisition it was a common charge against so-called witches that they had had intercourse with the devil; and of course with adequate torture many confessed to this sin. But I do not think that my lady of the Kikuyu village was a witch of this type. There is another group. Women who tend to have either the physical or psychological characteristics of men may come to be regarded as witches. This may happen to a woman with a glandular disorder so that she grows a beard, or to a woman with a psychological maladjustment which makes her personality re-semble that of a man. I think that there was something of this which gave the Kikuyu woman the magic power which she undoubtedly held.

We call these people witch-doctors, and because of the as-sociation with witch-craft, we tend to think in a loose kind of way that there is something evil about witch-doctors. I have no doubt that many witch-doctors have used their art for evil purposes, particularly in the way of bewitchment and the casting of spells. But I am equally sure that the majority of the African witch-doctors whom I met were well motivated and that their influence was predominantly a good one. It is said that native Africans with organic disease which is curable by modern medicine often go to witch-doctors and are thus denied effective treatment. This line of argument would be valid if alternative modern medical treatment were available, but in many cases this is simply not so. It seemed to me, as Africa is today, that the witch-doctors not only do much more good than harm to their patients, but also act as quite a potent stabilizing influence in the community.

My driver had heard of a witch-doctor in another Kikuyu village some miles distant. So before returning to Nairobi, we set off to find him. We eventually managed to track him down. He was a very old man. He had lost a leg, and his sight was poor.

I was immediately interested in his eyes which were quite grey in colour in contrast to the usual deep brown. I asked about this and was told that very old Africans often lose the brown pigment from their eyes which then become light grey.

This was quite a different type of witch-doctor, or perhaps he should not be called a witch-doctor at all. He was the wise

old man. Because of his age, it was held that he spoke with
wisdom. I cannot vouch for this, but in my talk with him
through an interpreter he certainly gave the impression of
shrewd cunning.

A Witch-Doctor who seemed Evil

My driver told me that Mackakos, a town some forty miles
from Nairobi, had quite a name for witch-doctors. He did not
know any himself; but he felt sure if we went there we could
find some. So we set off. As we were driving along I was surprised at seeing five or six giraffes not far from the road. The
driver thought it quite odd that I should be interested in them.
'Don't you have giraffes in Australia?'

We arrived at Mackakos, and drove to the market. The
driver asked me for some money, so that he could do some
shopping, and see what he could find out about the local
witch-doctors from chance contacts. I gave him a couple of
shillings and he left me. I wandered around on my own without anyone appearing to take undue interest in me. I noticed
a filthy, dirty, young woman calling out and begging from the
stall owners in very dramatic fashion. She was wild-eyed, and
her gesticulations seemed to express some terrible urgency.
This was the local idiot. I marvelled how tolerant people were
of her. Each would get rid of her firmly, but at the same time
in a kindly fashion. In our society she would have been quickly
put away. But these people could tolerate a disturbed person in
their midst without too much upset. This seemed to contrast
sharply with the families of many of my patients. Very often
they simply cannot bear to have a mentally sick relative with
them. I was thinking about this when she ran over to me, and
begged of me as she had of the others. I dared not give her
anything, so like the Pharisee I motioned her to be off, and
she soon left me.

The driver returned laden with vegetables and the news that
a very good witch-doctor lived only a few hundred yards away.
We found him in a house which was not only dirty but smelled
beyond description. He was sitting on the mud floor of the
passage-way treating a patient. After a few words with my
driver he went on with what he was doing. There was a small
fire of coals glowing in front of him in which he burned pieces

of horn. On one side of the fire he planted an ostrich feather in the earth floor; and on the other side he set up a figure which balanced and swayed back and forth on a small pedestal. The figure was in the form of a symbolic man about a foot in height. It was lightly balanced and continued to sway back and forth in hypnotic fashion. The driver acting as interpreter explained that the ostrich feather and the balancing figure were his spirits. The witch-doctor repeatedly took a mouthful of water from a jam tin and spat it out. Several times he poured water on the floor as a libation. Next he held a piece of paper over the fire until it was slightly charred. He then straightened out the paper, and showed us that some arabic writing had appeared on it. This was a message from the spirit of his great-great-great-grandfather. As if to convince us, he twice repeated the trick with the paper. He then spat on the fire in ritualistic fashion, and took snuff several times. Next he took a pink powdery substance from a cow-horn bottle, and put some on his right big toe, on his left cheek, and on the wall behind him. He then threw some of the pink substance on the opposite wall. This appeared to conclude the magic session.

I asked if he would show me what he had in a bag which he kept at his side. He opened it. In it there were numerous animal horns. Most of these had different things, such as feathers and cowrie shells, stuck in the hollow end with dried mud. He explained that these were used when the patient had been bewitched. There were also the feet of various animals and a lion's claw.

After leaving him my driver suggested that we should return and ask if he would tell our fortunes. The witch-doctor was quite pleased to do this, and repeated the whole ceremony with the ostrich feather and the balancing figure. A patient came back and sat beside us, and various children and other members of the household crammed into the narrow passage where we were seated. He then turned to me and asked through the driver if one of my relatives had something wrong with his leg. In actual fact my only brother had had a leg amputated some three months previously. His other pronouncements were either vague and oracular, or quite wrong.

In contrast to most of the other witch-doctors, this man seemed to have an evil atmosphere about him. But I am at a loss when I come to analyse why it should seem like that. Other witch-doctors had not seemed evil even when they did things such as making animal sacrifices, using magic, or throwing the bones. And others had had strange things such as dead bats and lizards about them; and they had not seemed evil. But this man did, quite definitely so.

Our mind receives very many messages which never pass the threshold of consciousness. Yet these messages of which we are quite unaware can still influence our judgements. This is very clearly proved in relation to subliminal advertising on the film screen and TV in which messages were flashed on the screen so quickly that the viewer had no conscious awareness that he had seen the message. Yet it affected his behaviour. In a similar way we probably observe many small things about a person without being aware of these observations. These may form the basis of such judgements as to whether we should think someone evil or not. Judgements of this nature are not subject to any conscious process of reason. But they are not illogical, rather they are paralogical. This is an explanation as to how we arrive at 'hunches'. And of course, they are very often right, although we cannot substantiate them by logical argument. This is how I explain my feeling about the witch-doctor at Mackakos.

A Witch-Doctor wants to Study under Me!

I flew from Nairobi to Entebbe; and following my usual custom hired a car with an English-speaking African driver. He soon told me about a very good witch-doctor whom he attended. He lived in quite a prosperous farmhouse a few miles from the town. The house was in modern European style. Nearby there were three or four traditional round huts which he used for seeing his patients. He was a big man in his early forties wearing a nondescript African gown. He spoke good English and said that he was guided in the treatment of his patients by the voices of the angels which he heard at night. He seemed rather disappointed that he never heard them during the day.

He told me that it was with the help of the angels that he had taught himself how to be a witch-doctor. He had had a good job with the government, but one night he had heard the angels telling him to become a witch-doctor. So he gave up his good job to devote himself to his new calling.

As a psychiatrist I see many patients who hear voices talking to them. Quite often it is the voices of angels which they claim to hear. These, of course, are the hallucinations which commonly occur in schizophrenia. So when the witch-doctor started talking about hearing the voices of the angels, I immediately thought that he was probably schizophrenic, and I watched carefully for other signs of the illness. But there were none. This intrigued me, as my patients who hear voices like this invariably show other signs of mental illness as well. There is often disharmony between the individual's thought and his feeling; this is shown in the way that the schizophrenic patient often smiles when he is telling you of something sad. But this man was quite normal in his emotional reactions. Nor was he suspicious, as many schizophrenics are, or he would not have told me about himself so openly. True, he had many strange ideas; but these could not be regarded as schizophrenic delusions as they were consistent with the culture in which he lived. A strange belief is only a delusion when it is in fact wrong, when it is not amenable to logical argument, and when it is not shared by others in the same culture. Thus the belief of a primitive person that the earth is flat is not a delusion. Although the things the witch-doctor was doing seemed odd when viewed by western standards, they were appropriate in themselves, and they had nothing of the impulsive quality which we so often see in the behaviour of schizophrenic patients. From all this, and the general manner and behaviour of the man, I concluded that he was not schizophrenic in spite of his hearing hallucinatory voices. I felt that this was yet another example of the strange by-ways of the mind, that in one set of circumstances it is quite normal for the mind to function in a certain way, yet to function in the same way in other circumstances is a sure sign of a terrible mental illness.

In answer to my questioning he explained that a very effective way of helping sick people was to send them away, and have them return with a fowl, some water from Lake Victoria, and a wooden cross. He then beheaded the fowl and allowed the blood to run over the patient. This was washed off with the water from Lake Victoria, and the wooden cross came into the ritual in some way which I did not quite follow. He made it clear that it was the voices of the angels which told him to do this, and not just spirit voices; so I gathered that he was a good Christian.

If a woman came to him because she could not have a baby, he would advise her to sleep with a spear beside her and to wear black. But her infertility may be due to her having been bewitched by another wife. This is done by magic after digging up a dead body. When the angels tell him this, he counters the bad magic with the ritual of beheading a fowl.

He demonstrated another method of treatment which he used. This was a matter of throwing the shells, which seemed to be a variation of throwing the bones which I had seen so often. They were cowrie shells which he himself had collected on the shores of Lake Victoria. Each shell had the peculiarity of having a natural hole in it.

We got on well together, and he asked me to write down my name for him. I did this. Then he asked for my address which I unthinkingly supplied.

We parted on good terms, and I returned to my hotel. The next morning I had my things packed, and was waiting on the veranda of the hotel for the bus to take me to the air-port. The hall-porter came and told me that Doctor So-and-So wished to see me. It was the witch-doctor of the previous day, dressed quite smartly in European clothes. Without any preliminaries, he told me that he was coming to Australia to study witch-doctoring under me! I realized that he probably had sufficient money to make the trip, as many of the witch-doctors charge exorbitantly high fees. A man might be charged an amount equal to a whole year's income to be relieved of his bewitchment. I told him that Australia was a very long way away. But he was not deterred. Then I told him that it was often very cold in Melbourne, where I live, and that I was sure he would not like it. But he was set on coming at all costs.

I was beginning to panic. The bus would arrive at any moment. I felt that I must act quickly. I would show him some-thing now, and then he would be satisfied. We were sitting on the veranda of the hotel. Other passengers awaiting the bus were only a few yards away.

I told him, 'Look at me. Look at me. You are relaxed. You have never heard the angels speak to you in the daytime. Look at me. Listen. Listen carefully. You can hear them speaking now.'

And he did hear the angels speaking to him. He was over-joyed. But instead of being satisfied with what I had shown him, he wanted more; and his resolve to come to Australia to study witch-doctoring under me was more than ever fixed in his mind. I thought I would try more hypnosis with a different slant to it. Just then the bus arrived. I had to go. I kept saying, 'I wouldn't come to Australia.' He kept saying how good it would be to be with me in Australia. I had to take my seat. The bus moved off, and that was that.

It has not happened yet. But I keep feeling that it might happen any day.

The Copts

I am too much of a dreamer. I went to Addis Ababa full of romantic notions. Here I would find the mystique of the Copts, and see them practise a form of Christianity which has remained practically unchanged since the early days of the Christian era.

But I was overwhelmed by the squalor of the place. Here there is poverty and filth which seemed worse than anything I had seen even in India. A medical professor told me that somewhere between forty and sixy percent of the population suffer from venereal disease in the form of gonorrhoea, and that in one province ten percent of the people have leprosy. In Ethiopia, in the whole of the country, there is not a single city which is sewered. In the main street of Addis Ababa men openly urinate in the gutters. Their only concern is that the sun should not shine on their organ lest it give them gonorrhoea! This is their widespread belief. Bare-footed men, women and children stagger unsteadily under enormous loads of eucalyptus shoots which are used as fuel for cooking. The city itself is split up by a number of small ravines in the depths of which there is squalor unspeakable. This is the background of Ethiopia where only five percent of the people can read and write. A leading educationalist talked of the great strides in education that were being made. I could not understand what he meant, until he explained that prior to 1945 there was not a single school in the whole country! We often think of the backwardness of heathen countries, but this is the state of development of a country which has been Christian since the fourth century.

A couple of weeks later in Cairo I met a young American couple. The man told me that they were on their way to Addis Ababa for two years. He was going to teach business methods at the university. I really felt incensed, not at him, but at the appalling lack of judgement of those who administer aid to the under-developed countries. In recent years it has become

quite an 'in' thing to have worked in an under-developed
country for a short time. Whether or not the country gets
much help from the project seems to be a secondary consideration. But the idea of spending public money on sending men
to teach business methods at a university level in a country
where ninety-five percent of the people can neither read nor
write, and who are in urgent need of sanitation and basic medical care, seems quite incomprehensible to me.

While I was there I wanted to see what I could of the Copts.
The old church was a strange place. It was built in the form
of an inner shrine within the main building. A service was
being held in this outer part. Priests were chanting an endless
liturgy. It went on and on. Both the priests and the small con-
gregation seemed half hypnotized by the sing-song repetition
of the sacred words. I am told that few understand the mean-
ng of the words, but it was clear that all understood the mean-
ng of the incantation as a mysterious participation in the worship of God. They stood because there were no pews; but each
person had a straight thin stick about five feet in length. These
are capped with a metal fork, something like the traditional
shepherd's crook. The worshippers stand with their sticks in
front of them with their hands resting on the fork. The chin
is then rested on the hands and they remain propped up in
this way, with the stick taking much of their weight. It seemed
an extraordinarily disrespectful attitude for a church service,
but supported in this way, the worshippers are able to remain
standing for services of great length.

Many of the priests have little education, and people who
follow the Christian Coptic church often retain a primitive
belief in spirits. This is more so in the country than in the
cities. I was driving along a main road some thirty miles from
Addis Ababa, when we came to a great crowd of people on
the road. My driver told me it was a funeral. The service had
to be held on the road because it was the only dry place, as this
was the wet season and the fields were all half under water. As
we approached I could see that there was a great commotion
with people milling around in all directions. There were ten
or a dozen horsemen galloping wildly up and down the centre
of the road with the crowd on either side. I could hear rifle
shots. Then as we came to the crowd I could see what was
happening. The horsemen were wild-eyed in a kind of a frenzy,
sweat was pouring from their horses. Several of them carried

rifles which they kept waving about and firing into the air as they galloped. To watch this was quite a terrifying experience. Other horsemen who did not have rifles carried long sticks with which they kept beating the air. All this was to drive off wicked spirits which might be associating with the body of the dead man. I persuaded my driver to stop in the middle of the gathering. No one took any notice of us. The crowd was weeping and moaning and showing all the outward signs of grief; while the horsemen kept galloping past the car firing their rifles. This was real frenzy. They were frightening off the evil spirits, but at the same time they themselves had become possessed. Never have I seen anything quite like it.

Casting out Devils with a Garden Hose

At Wollasso, some fifty or sixty miles from Addis Ababa, there is a man widely famed for his healing by exorcism of devils. The healer is a bishop of the Coptic church. He is a big, imposing man with a beard, and a golden crucifix hangs on his chest over his black robes. It was a Sunday when I visited him, and he explained that he worked at exorcism on every day except Sundays which he kept free for a religious service. He explained in detail the exact procedure of ridding a patient of devils. His description was confirmed by a doctor, who was a frequent visitor to his healing sessions.

He showed me the place where he worked. It was a large ramshackle shed. There was a formal pulpit, and pews were arranged as in a church. At the back there was an old forty-four gallon drum which had been filled with water from a well in the yard. Attached to the forty-four gallon drum was a hand pump and a long length of garden hose. This led into an extension of the shed at the side of the pulpit. It is here that the exorcism takes place. Men and women patients strip to the waist. The bishop takes the nozzle of the hose in one hand and a large wooden cross in the other. A boy gets to work on the hand pump, and the bishop hoses the patient. At the same time he calls upon the devil to come out. The devil, in the voice of the patient, usually answers back, 'I won't come out, I won't come out.' Then in the name of the Lord, the bishop commands the devil in a loud voice to leave his victim. Sometimes the devil uses the patient's voice to jeer at the bishop.

Then force has to be used. As the devil speaks these profane words, the bishop gets to him by squirting the patient in the mouth. Sometimes he has to flog the devil out of the patient with heavy blows from his large wooden cross. If it seems that the devil is inhabiting the victim's head, he bangs the patient on the head with the cross. The devil is eventually defeated, and is anxious to leave the body of his victim. In the struggle of the devil to leave his body, the patient is frequently thrown on the floor, and often has a convulsive seizure. The bishop told me of a recent case in which he had driven no less than seven devils from the body of a patient, each time with the same effect.

He showed me long lists of patients who had been success-fully treated. He said that over a great number of years some sixty thousand patients had come to him. Then he showed me literally thousands upon thousands of charms which pat-ients had been wearing without effect, and which they had left with him, when he had cured them by casting out their devil. The charms were tied up in bundles of forty or fifty and were left hanging from nails around the sides of the building. In corners there were piles of sticks and crutches which had been left by those whose lameness had been cured.

The whole scene seemed just too fantastic – a little black boy working the hand pump at the old drum of water, and the bishop in black robes and golden crucifix hosing out devils and banging the patients on the head with his wooden cross. Yet I know of no psychiatrist who could produce such tangible evidence of success. A partial explanation lies in the fact that the form in which nervous illness manifests itself is to some extent dependent on cultural influences. A good example of this is the way in which nervous illness in the first world war showed itself in cardiac symptoms in a condition which be-came known as D.A.H. – Disordered Action of the Heart. In the second world war this condition was practically unknown, and nervous illness was manifested predominantly in dyspeptic symptoms and open anxiety. Primitive peoples tend to mani-fest nervous illness in hysterical symptoms such as paralysis of limbs. This type of hysteria is often relieved quite easily by any dramatic method of treatment. In our culture the authoritative use of hypnosis or the intravenous injection of a barbiturate drug is often used. The main problem is that, if the symptom is just removed in this way without anything being done to relieve the underlying anxiety which causes the symptom, there is a likelihood of other symptoms arising. I do not know anything of the relapse rate among the bishop's patients, but by any standards he must surely be regarded as one of the great healers of modern times, even if he does work among people whose nervous illness is relatively easily relieved by dramatic methods.

By the time he had finished explaining all this to me, people were beginning to file into the shed and seat themselves on the pews. They were coming for his Sunday afternoon service. It was a motley crowd, if ever there was one. Most of the people were poor, because nearly everyone in Ethiopia is poor. But when people are both poor and sick there is real destitution. Yet in the crowd there was a sprinkling of well-dressed men and women. Some were obviously very ill, and came in supported by others on each side of them. Some were carried in, and two or three were brought along on stretchers. The bishop, with me at his side, stood by the pulpit. Many came up to him, and he offered them his crucifix to kiss. A chair was brought for me and placed in front of the pulpit. The bishop mounted the steps to the pulpit and commenced the service. There were some hymns and a long sermon in which he maintained the attention of all who were present. As I was unable to understand a word of what he was saying, I sat there absorbed by the facial expressions of those before me. There, in those ramshackle surroundings, listening to a man whose theological concepts seemed tawdry in the extreme, I saw hope and calm in the faces of those who were otherwise destitute. He was confident. He knew no doubts. Nor did he know humility. In fact, he had a childish conceit about him. But in spite of his conceit there was obvious sincerity. He has helped a hundred times as many patients as I shall ever help in my professional life. And for this I respect him.

Life as Preparation for Death

In the past hundred years everyone who has travelled has been to Egypt, and more books have been written on the wonders of Egypt than on most other places. But there is a number of different aspects to the wonders of Egypt. Some travellers marvel at the grandeur of the monuments; others ponder as to how they were constructed, others wonder at the meaning of the hieroglyphs, and still others at the organization of a society which could produce such things. But for me, by far the greatest wonder is the purpose behind it all. What is the meaning of all this? I do not refer to the translation of the hieroglyphs or the purpose of the pyramids. I refer to the meaning of the ancient Egyptian way of life; a way of life that above all else was focused on preparation for life after death.

It is not the idea of preparing for life after death which is so strange, but rather the way they went about it. After all, the preparation for a life after death is quite a part of Christian teaching, and the idea of 'pie in the sky' is common enough. Christians believe in the resurrection of the body. So did the Egyptians, particularly so for their ruling classes. But they aimed to achieve this by the physical preservation of the body through mummification, and an elaborate system of magic ritual. By this means they not only assured themselves of life after death; but like many Christians, they assured themselves of survival in very comfortable circumstances.

Let me go back a stage further in our line of reasoning. What drives a people to invent such an elaborate system of magic, with its great temples, strange shaped gods and mystical burial ceremonies? The answer is simple. It is our fear of death, of the unknown. And of course this is a basic cause of the anxiety which seems to be an almost universal attribute of man.

You and I have the same problem, but we approach it differently. The Egyptians used the psychological mechanism of magic ritual, we use another psychological method. In general, we deny the problem. In our culture men and women in normal mental health hardly think of death. By this very simple means we avoid much of this basic anxiety. We worry about hundreds of minor problems. But not death. And strangely enough many of these minor problems, which cause us so much concern, are like death in that we cannot do anything about them. Our denial of the major problem is so complete, and in general so effective, that we have come to regard it as natural that we should not think of death. It is taboo, and the subject is avoided in general conversation.

Perhaps we could learn from this. We do not want to lead a life centred on death like the ancient Egyptians. But on the other hand, our taboo on the discussion of death must make the problem more difficult for us when we ultimately have to face it.

Old Symbols in a New Setting

Of all the Egyptian hieroglyphs the eye symbol is the most readily discernible. It immediately arrests the attenion of the casual observer. This is the Eye of Ra, the 'oujat' eye, or the Eye of Horus. It is seen everywhere in the hieroglyphic writing on both monuments and on the walls of the tombs. But the same symbol has also frequently occurred in the paintings of schizophrenic patients whom I have treated. And even more remarkable, the meaning which the schizophrenic patients gave to the symbol was essentially the same as that of the Egyptian eye, although the patients had no knowledge of Egyptology.

The Egyptian mythology of the Eye is extremely complex. The Eye may represent different gods and different forces at the same time. And what makes it even more baffling, at times it develops an individuality of its own. The Great God sent his Eye on an errand. But when the Eye returned he found his place taken by another, either the sun or the moon. This caused the wrath of the Eye. It then became the Great Goddess and the scourge of mankind.

This, in effect, is just what my schizophrenic patients said of the eyes they painted. The eye was God, watching them, looking into their faults, scourging them, driving them on. It would seem that the ancient Egyptians had a sense of guilt just as we do. They expressed it in their religious mythology and ritual as the eye of Ra persecuting them. And some four thousand years later my schizophrenic patients expressed the same idea in the same symbolism.

The feeling of guilt is something very deep within us. We feel that God or some power is watching us, and sees all our faults. This is related to conscience. It persecutes us. It drives us down the straight and narrow path however much we would like to digress to other fields. This accounts for the failure of rationalist systems of conduct to allay our innate sense of guilt. We can understand at a logical level that there is no occasion for us to feel guilty about some particular matter, but we still do. All of us at one time or another must surely have had this experience. The guilt lies deep within us. It is not accessible to logical argument. It is only allayed by paralogical means such as the magic rituals of ancient Egypt.

There are many strange things about symbolism. I once had a schizophrenic patient who painted a number of pictures showing a bird flying away from a figure which represented herself. When I asked her about this, she explained that the bird was her soul leaving her body. It was only recently that I came to learn that a bird, quite distinct from the falcon-headed Horus, represents the soul in Egyptian hieroglyphics. Strange indeed, that my schizophrenic patient should use the same symbolism.

The symbol shaped like a tennis racquet with a line drawn across it is one of the commonest hieroglyphs. This is 'ankh'. It is the symbol of life. Gods are often shown holding it in their hand, or bestowing it upon a dead pharoah. If we examine the symbol in the light of Freudian psychopathology we see that the 'ankh' is a complex sexual symbol. It combines both the projecting symbol of the male and the hollow female symbol. So in these terms it is easy enough to see why it should have such magic qualities, and be regarded as the symbol of life itself.

But the 'ankh' also enters into a different grade of symbolism. Shortly after leaving Egypt I went to Paris. At the Louvre there was a display of early Coptic paintings. I noticed that in the corner of one of these religious paintings there was a cross. But it was not a cross. It was 'ankh'. It had the upper segment expanded into the tennis racquet shape which we see everywhere in the Egyptian hieroglyphic writing. 'Ankh' is the symbol of life, but with Christians the cross has come to express the same idea. The early Coptic painting showed a fusion of the two symbols in a way that is not at all uncommon in the history of symbolism.

A similar principle is demonstrated in one of the best known stories of Egyptian mythology. We have our Christian belief. The Christ-God was slain by the powers of evil. He was crucified, dead and buried, but on the third day he rose again from the dead. And so the pattern was set for individual resurrection. But this was no new concept. Osiris was killed by his wicked brother Set who symbolizes evil. But his wife, Isis, searched and found all the remnants of his dismembered body. She then pieced them together and restored him to life. He then returned to the land of the dead to welcome the soul of others, and reign over those who have died. Thus man had evolved the concept of the resurrection of the body long before the advent of Christian teaching.

Mystery in Egyptian Religion

There is mystery in religion; and nowhere is this more clearly shown than in the religion of the ancient Egyptians. But the modern trend is to take the mystery out of religion. Everywhere religion is being rationalized. We see this particularly in the Protestant churches. This process follows the development of science and the ever-increasing emphasis on the use of the logical faculties of the mind. But religion deals essentially with paralogical mental processes where the simple cold facts of logic have little relevance.

When religion is robbed of its mystery it loses its power. When I say this I do not speak from the standpoint of theology, of which I have little knowledge; but I speak as a psychiatrist, who has seen many patients disturbed with religious problems. Experience with these patients has shown that a rationalist approach, which has seemed adequate and satisfying when the patient has been well, breaks down when the patient is under the stress of nervous illness. Of course, the faith of people with a mystical approach to religion may also fail in these circumstances. But my clinical experience with patients suggests that this happens much less frequently than with those who have rationalized their religious beliefs.

There are two great classes of nervous illness, the psychoses which involve the patient's sanity, and the psychoneuroses in which the sanity is not affected. Religious belief would seem to offer little protection against psychotic illness, but it may be of great help to the patient who suffers from psychoneurotic or psychosomatic conditions. I would not presume to know how this comes about. Some sick people have told me quite openly that they feel that they are given strength, both of the mind and the body, by the personal intervention of the Almighty. Others do not go as far as this. They may say that they have faith, and that this gives them understanding so that they can meet their present difficulties in a calm and philosophical state of mind. This approach is undoubtedly a great help in the stress of nervous illness.

There are, however, other patients whose attitude of mind would seem to approximate more closely to that of the ancient Egyptians in the way in which they maintain little rituals in their everyday life. Anxiety, in the form of inner tension, is one of the great problems of mankind. Different people evolve different means of coping with anxiety. Thus some avoid situations which might produce anxiety. Others allay their anxiety with alcohol or drugs. Some become brash and assertive to avoid feeling anxious. Still others avoid anxiety by having everything just right. These are the perfectionists. If everything is just right there can be nothing to worry about. So everything is kept neat and tidy and in order. But this way of keeping everything orderly may become a kind of ritual. The individual is more at ease if he does things just the same way as he did them last time. By doing things in a certain way he feels less tense within himself. He often realizes that these fixed patterns of doing things are illogical, but he continues in the pattern because of the ease that it brings to his mind. In a small way the pattern of doing this becomes a kind of magic ritual. This might apply to the way he takes off his clothes and puts them away, or to the particular way he washes himself, or it may involve not touching certain things which have been touched by others. The person concerned often gives good reasons why he does these things. He may say that if you are neat and tidy you know where things are. But he cannot explain why he has to spend ten minutes doing it when a couple of seconds would suffice. In other words, many of us, perhaps most of us, have this tendency to develop magic rituals in very much the same way as the Egyptians developed theirs.

We have a greater tendency to develop magic rituals when we are under stress. For instance, during the war many airmen who came back from a dangerous mission felt more at ease if they wore the same clothes again on their next mission. This often applied particularly to some scarf or sweater. The garment became a lucky charm. It helped the man to feel easier in himself. In fact it developed magic qualities. In the same way, if there were any particular threat to the Egyptians, either by war or famine, the people turned to the priests to pay special attention to the sacred rituals.

But there is more to it than the lessening of anxiety by magic ritual. There is the symbolism. We use symbols in our everyday life. The printed letters are the symbol for the word; and the word in turn is the symbol for the object or idea. This is a very simple form of symbolism. On a more complex scale, the cross symbolizes the death of Jesus; but in certain circumstances the symbol can acquire some of the properties of the idea which it symbolizes. This introduces the magic of symbolism. The Christian church believes that the bread taken in the communion service not only symbolizes the body of Christ, but is in fact his body. This is the type of meaning which we must give the Egyptian symbols in order to understand them. Then we can feel how life after death is attained, and at the same time present anxiety is allayed.

An Unpleasant Experience in Moscow

I had flown from Australia to India and thence via Taschkent
to Moscow. The flight itself had been rather eerie. On leaving
New Delhi I was the only first-class passenger in the huge
'Aeroflot' plane. The tourist class was crammed full; but I was
there by myself in uneasy isolation. It was called first class, but
it lacked the ordinary comfort of the usual tourist accom-
modation. We took off at dawn, and as soon as we were away,
I was offered caviar and vodka by a huge air-hostess. This was
my first introduction to Russian womanhood. She was really
terrific. The muscles rippled under her uniform. But even for
her I was simply unable to face either caviar or vodka at seven
o'clock in the morning. After that she left me, and did not
come near me again for the remainder of the flight. I could
only presume that this is a sign of her righteous indignation
at my bourgeois tendencies.

This was in 1960, not long after the sensational shooting
down of the American U2 spy plane, and the subsequent trial
of the unfortunate pilot. Things were difficult in Moscow,
especially for anyone travelling by himself without affiliation
with any government body. All arrangements had to be made
through the official 'Entourist' agency, and on arrival I was
taken to a hotel of their choice where most of the visiting
foreigners were housed.

The purpose of my visit to Moscow was simple enough. I
wished to meet, and talk about technical matters with some
doctors whom I knew to be working with hypnosis in a rather
similar way to myself. I had written to one of these men,
and had received a very friendly letter in reply saying that he
was looking forward to meeting me. I also had with me a
letter from a friend, an English doctor who had been in Moscow on official business a short time previously. My friend
was a sensible man who knew just what I might want. He
gave me in his letter a list of names and addresses of five or
six doctors in Moscow who might help me. After each name

he had added a short paragraph describing the person. 'This chap is very good on such and such, but knows damn all about this and that.' 'He is all right in medicine, but only wants to talk politics.' 'This fellow is an old fool, but he could introduce you to other people in your field.' In fact they were helpful little notes about each individual; and at the end he gave me their telephone numbers. This again was intended to be helpful as telephone directories are rare in Russia and are usually only accessible to officials.

Soon after arrival I asked the guide who was allotted to me if she would please telephone the Moscow doctor who had written to me. I gave her his telephone number on my list. She seemed surprised at this. She was hesitant; and then she became very definite.

'I cannot ring him up until tomorrow.'

This will appear foolish to anyone who has not had the experience of being bullied by a guide from the official 'Entourist' agency. It did not matter what I said, she simply would not budge. However, she knew that I was a psychiatrist, and insisted on making appointments for me to see two or three important people in this branch of medicine. This seemed to me some kind of appeasement for not contacting the man whom I wished to see.

Next morning I asked her again if she would phone him for me. She became rather aggressive and said she would do so after lunch. And so it went on for two or three days. I tried myself to use a phone in the hotel; but of course it was hopeless as the operator could only speak Russian. So I forced the guide to come with me to the phone in the hotel lobby, and I told her to get the number without further delay. She refused and said it could only be done from the head office of the 'Entourist' agency. I was getting very tired and cross about it all. So I bundled her into a taxi and told her to take me to the agency. When we arrived she asked me for his telephone number. I folded the letter so that it just showed the doctor's name and number, whereupon she snatched the letter from me and ran off with it. I tried to follow her, but was immediately stopped by a guard. I protested loudly to the guards and the people behind the counter but they only shook their heads and raised their hands to indicate that they did not speak English. I was irritated further by the tell-tale changes of expression which showed me that at least two of them understood every word I said. So I was just left there. In about ten minutes the guide returned. I held out my hand for my letter. She just shook her head. The only explanation I could get from her was, 'They have to have it. Then they will ring up for you.'

I made a great fuss. She eventually said she would go back and get the letter. She went off. I tried to follow, but was prevented. In twenty minutes or so she returned with it, saying that they could not telephone my friend today.

It seemed obvious that the letter had been copied or photographed. I thought of all the apt little comments that my English friend had made about the Moscow doctors.

I was quite distressed about all this. I thought that at least I should report it. So I went to the Embassy. The ambassador was out of Moscow. The young man who was in charge was only interested in telling me about a party he had had with some fellow countryman of mine a few days previously.

I had a whole week in Moscow, and in spite of all my efforts, I was prevented from meeting the people whom I wanted to see. The nearest I got to it was one day when the guide would not telephone my friend and I persuaded her to drive me to his address. We eventually came to a house. She got out, but she and the driver would not let me leave the car. After some time she returned, and told me that he was not there. I expect she read on my face that I did not believe her. She then explained that she would take me instead to see a very important psychiatrist.

It all seemed very strange. I am in no way active politically. Why should anyone wish to interfere with me? The only reason I could think of concerned brain-washing. Just at that time, the trial of the American U2 pilot had stirred up quite an interest in brain-washing in the press throughout the world. I had published books and articles on hypnosis. The doctors whom I had wanted to see were working in this field. The only possible explanation for the official concern about my movements seemed to be that I was suspected of being interested in their methods of scientific brain-washing.

The Old and the New in Medicine

Although my guide from the 'Entourist' agency mastered me completely, and effectively prevented me from contacting the doctors whom I wanted to see, she did in fact provide several interesting introductions. Each time she took me on one of these visits, we always seemed to pass the hall where the American U2 pilot had been tried, and each time I had to listen to her version of all the political implications of the incident. All day and every day, if there were a lull in our conversation, she would ask, 'Why are the Americans trying to start a third world war?' I would explain that I am not an American, and that there are many matters of American foreign policy with which I would disagree; but there was one thing about which I was sure, that America was not trying to start another war. At first I accepted her refusal to listen to me just as a facet of the 'party line', and I took little notice of it. But as I saw more of her I came to realize that this was more than just the 'party line', and that she really believed what she said when she told me that America was trying to start a world war. I realized the awful significance of her attitude. If one really believes that one is about to be attacked, the obvious thing to do is to get in first, and make a surprise attack oneself. This is surely one of our greatest dangers.

She arranged for me to meet the head of a famous research institute. He was pleasant and co-operative, and showed me some advanced neurophysiological experiments of the utmost delicacy. I explained to him that these were matters quite beyond my comprehension; and without giving details, I told him that I had been unable to meet the people whom I had wanted to see. I thought that he would be cross at this, and feel that he was wasting his time with me. But no. He became even more friendly and sympathetic. Neither of us discussed the matter further; but it was clear that he understood the situation. He seemed a little sad. He ordered sandwiches and champagne to be brought to his room. He clinked his glass with mine. 'To friendship between our countries.' It was rather sad; he knew it, and I knew it too.

The next day my guide took me to meet the director of a large psychiatric hospital. He was very intense, and talked to me across a large desk on which I noticed a recent issue of the *Lancet*. He kept his eyes firmly on mine. They had a kind of fanaticism about them. I thought if I were sick I would not like such a man as my doctor. Then very deliberately, and speaking very slowly so as to be sure that I understood the full meaning of what he said, 'Of course, there is no psychoneurosis in this country. Psychoneurosis is a disease of capitalist society. We simply do not have psychoneurotic patients.' And all the time he gazed with almost unbelievable intensity into my eyes.

I was naturally taken aback by such a statement. I started to protest, 'But . . .'. However he quickly interrupted, 'We have alcoholism. And in five years we shall have mastered that. But psychoneurosis, no. It is only a disease of capitalist society.'

Here was an informed man making a careful statement which was manifestly untrue. I read the message of the fire in his eyes which told me, 'Don't discuss this further.' So I asked him about alcoholism. He was obviously glad that I had avoided a head-on collision.

But I kept wondering, 'Why such a lie? Why the self-delusion? Why bring it out in the first sentence of our conversation?'

He talked on about the war, particularly about the fanatical courage of the people in the defence of Stalingrad; how they made ramparts of the bodies of the dead, and how the seriously wounded refused to leave the lines. Then it began to dawn on me. Such people could not possibly suffer from psychoneurosis. And this extraordinary intensity about him was a kind of psychological defence, lest he might remember that the heroes of Stalingrad were also human, and suffered the ordinary ills of humanity.

The sequel to his denial of psychoneurotic illness in Russia came a couple of days later. I was taken to a recently opened polyclinic. It was all new, and everyone was obviously very proud of it.

With two or three other foreigners I was taken to a small lecture room and the purpose of the clinic was explained to us. During the talk several large women dressed in untidy white overalls came in and sat down. I thought that this was the classless society in operation, and that these were the charwomen who had come in to hear what the boss had to say. But I was wrong. I later discovered that they were women doctors; although I would never have guessed from their appearance. In Russia, medicine is a woman's profession. I was told that sixty percent of all Russian doctors are women, but among medical students the percentage is ninety.

Then I was shown around the clinic. Here was both my dis-

S.P.S.T.   F

illusionment and my enlightenment. I saw workers being treated for sore muscles and strained backs by hydrotherapy and mud packs. These are forms of treatment which have been outmoded in western medicine for more than half a century! I thought of the research experiments which I had seen at the institute a few days previously. These were at the very forefront of medicine. But these advances had not found their way to everyday treatment. Instead people were treated with hot and cold showers and mud baths. Then it all became clear to me. These are the psychoneurotic patients, only they are given another name. In a society where a condition of anxiety is something shameful, the unconscious mind modifies the usual symptoms of nervous illness; and instead of tension and apprehension, the patient suffers from pains in the back and other muscles.

Then I was taken to another department. The attitude of the man who was showing us around made it clear that he was keeping the best for the last, 'Now I shall show you our acupuncture department.' I could hardly believe the words. Acupuncture is a form of traditional Chinese medicine which has been practised in that country for many centuries. It consists of inserting very fine needles into the affected part. In ancient China the needles were splinters of bamboo, now they are made of metal. The head of the department, through an interpreter, told me how this method of treatment had recently been imported from China. He showed me the acupuncture needles. They are of flexible steel wire, and vary in length from a quarter of an inch to about two and a half inches. Each has a little metal handle about half an inch long which allows the operator to take hold of the needle and also prevents it from slipping completely into the tissues. I was told that this method of treatment was used for a great variety of conditions. Treatment may involve the insertion of five or six needles or up to twenty, thirty or more. The needles are left in place for a varying length of time, usually about twenty minutes. Treatment is repeated daily until the patient is better.

The medical theory behind this treatment is that acupuncture works by providing counter-irritation. The long needles are inserted quite slowly, and the flexibility of the needle allows it to slide around nerves and blood vessels without doing too much harm.

Here was a centuries old form of treatment being used in

the newest polyclinic in Moscow. What a far cry from the really stupendous advances in research which are being made in that country. And of course it all fits in with the idea that there is no psychoneurosis in Russia. A worker will not complain too much about his nerves, but he can have a bad back without feeling ashamed of it. And twenty or thirty needles stuck into his back each day would certainly encourage the worker to return to his job. And I thought of my own patients. This is something different from the kindness, sympathy and understanding of traditional Christian medicine. So also is the routine Russian treatment of alcoholics in which the patient is repeatedly made to drink alcohol and is then given an injection to make him vomit. This is continued until he develops a loathing of alcohol. This is undoubtedly achieved, but only at cost to the individual's personality.

We were about to leave the department. The interpreter had already gone through the door. There was only myself and the head of the department left in the room. I knew he could not speak English. I picked up two of his needles, one short one and one long one. I carefully showed them to him and said, 'You do not mind if I take just these two.' He obviously did mind. But I could not understand Russian. So I smiled sweetly at him as I put them in my pocket, and followed the guide out the door. Since then many of my medical colleagues have marvelled at my little souvenirs, as they have scarcely been able to believe that such treatment is used in present day Russia.

An Art Show – Russian Style

Whatever one's views about art, there must be one thing that is certain; art means something. As to exactly what it does mean different people have different ideas; but because it does mean something, it must represent some aspect of the thought and feeling of those who create it. That is why I like going to art shows, to try to find out what people are thinking and feeling. Perhaps you are inclined to disagree with this general idea. You might point out that many artists are individualists, and as such their work does not reflect the sentiments of those around them. But I do not think they are such complete individualists as they think they are. I believe that these artists are people who have the ability to give expression to the uncrystallized thoughts and feelings of others. These are the sentiments that are just forming in the minds of ordinary men and women, and of which they are not yet aware. It is easy to see this trend in forms of art that have some reference to the social and political development of the day. But the idea applies in much more subtle ways than this. We see it, of course, in the way that art reflects our attitude towards sex, and more generally, man's attitude towards women. But we can see it also in the way that art reflects our way of looking at things. Is the world bleak and ugly, or is it full of wonder and beauty? Must man be hard and cruel, or can he be kind and loving? Is he a worthless automaton driven on by psychological and social forces which he does not understand, or is there within him some spark of an inner spirit which enlightens and ennobles all that is around him? This I believe is the meaning which the artist expresses in his work.

But this is more than just the artist giving expression to his personal ideas. If his work did not represent the unformed views of a proportion of the people of his culture, no one would look at his work, no one would go to his exhibitions. He would not be known; he simply would not make the grade as an artist.

So when my guide announced that she was taking me to a great exhibition of pictures, I was very pleased; although I would have been even more pleased if she had given me the opportunity to say 'yes' or 'no'.

It was a great exhibition; of that there is no doubt. But it was something quite different from any exhibition of paintings which I have ever seen.

It was assembled to commemorate twenty years of union of the Baltic countries with Russia. The paintings were of great strength, great vividness and clarity. Nothing was left to the imagination. There was only one theme. All of those hundreds of paintings expressed the striving of the workers for freedom against the oppressive fear of capitalism. Yet the pictures were no mere posters. I would not have thought it possible that the same theme could be depicted in so many different ways. There was great strength and vitality about it all. The idea of striving was continually represented, not only striving against capitalism, but men striving together in the fields and in the factories for greater material output. In all this there was the idea of unity and pulling together. And I thought how similar t was to the way these ideas were presented in my school-day games. And with it there was the idea of men and women striving together. It was inspiring. And I was inspired by it.

In many pictures there was the face of Lenin in the background, with the workers looking to him to gain new strength 'or their struggle. In this it followed the pattern of all that body of Christian art which shows people turning to another 'ace for strength in another struggle.

In every picture the ideas were represented realistically. Men and women are striving in field and factory. In the whole exhibition there was not a single abstract painting.

As I have said, it was inspiring; but it was terrifying too. I was not terrified by the awful and single-minded presentation of class war. We are all too familiar with the idea to be terrified by it any longer. But what was terrifying was the thought that in the whole of this great exhibition there was not one single expression of tender emotion. Strength, unity and striving, but of love or tenderness there was no thought. Imagine a great exhibition in Paris, or even London or New York without reference to love or sex. This exhibition in Moscow showed men and women together; but they were always men fighters and women fighters, never men and women together in the way that we like to think.

The people at the exhibition were all most enthusiastic. They were inspired just as I was. I could see this in their faces. But I am sure they did not feel the terror behind it all, this open expression of lack of the most precious quality of man.

Disappointment in Taipei

For some years I have been interested in Buddhism, not only in the philosophy itself, but also in the practical matter that there may be something about the meditative state which could be adapted for use in modern psychiatry. At the time, I thought that I had gone as far as I could with books, and I felt that my only chance of gaining something useful would be by personal contact with an exponent of Buddhist practices. By good fortune I had been able to obtain a letter of introduction to a university professor in Taiwan who was not only a Buddhist scholar and personally active in Buddhist practices, but who also spoke good English. I was on my way back to Australia from a medical meeting in Europe, and I flew from Hong Kong to Taiwan especially to meet him.

First, I was invited to see their psychiatric department at the university. This was just what I had hoped for. Here I would see the integration of the wisdom of age-old Buddhism and the learning of modern psychiatry. Just what I wanted! But no. What I was shown was just a little America in a far away place. It was all new; and they were so proud of it. Every detail was a replica of the same sterile, standardized, psychiatric set-up that one sees all over America. And they told me with pride that many of their staff had had first hand experience of psychiatry in America itself.

I enquired about treatment. This slavishly followed the stereotyped lines of American psychiatry. I gingerly asked about the Buddhist background of the patients, and whether Buddhist practice was in any way a help in nervous illness. But my enquiry was hardly taken seriously. They had turned away from their traditional cultural heritage; and as they quizzed me about recent developments in western psychiatry, I could see how they prided themselves in their modern scientific approach.

I was disappointed in that I had failed to find what I was seeking – some kind of integration of the basic teachings of

Buddhist philosophy and western psychiatry. But more than ever, I was sad at their uncritical acceptance of western psychiatry, and their attempt to transplant it holus-bolus into surroundings where it is not completely suited. This seems to be the pattern of things. There is much that is good in our culture, and it seems a pity that the Asian is not more selective in what he imports. But the same applies to ourselves. At the present time we have quite a vogue of yoga. But in general we have imported only the gloss and the tinsel, and the basic teaching has largely eluded us.

When I could get him to myself, my friend the Buddhist scholar spoke openly of his practices. He had been brought up on the teachings of Buddha, but in adolescence had turned to Christianity for several years, only to return once more to his original Buddhist faith more firmly than ever. Here was a man of unique experience in the matters in which I was so interested. I tried to ascertain the reasons for his changes of faith. But of course he could not tell me clearly. Changes of faith are not made in response to logical reasoning, but come about as the result of paralogical activity of the mind in ways such as suggestion and intuition. He found that Buddhism was more satisfying to him; and he kept emphasizing to me that since his return to Buddhism he had been much less tense and anxious. This may well have been so, but as I saw him, he was still far from real calm and ease, and showed many of the common signs of open anxiety. He thought that meditation was a great help in the relief of nervous tension. I was pleased to hear him say this, as I often teach my tense patients autohypnosis, which they practise in a way that is not altogether dissimilar to Buddhist meditation. Furthermore, he felt that the typical Christian preoccupation with feelings of guilt added considerably to the individual's degree of nervous tension. With this, I was in complete accord.

Every now and then, perhaps every five or six months or so, if he found himself getting tense again, he would visit his teacher who lived the life of a hermit in the mountains. Unlike most of the Buddhist masters, his teacher was a woman. He explained that on these occasions she would correct his posture for meditation. This is a matter which I am still not able to understand. Buddhists and yogis alike place great emphasis on the correct squatting position. I can appreciate the importance of being well balanced if one is to maintain a certain position for a long time. I can also understand the necessity to be slightly uncomfortable so that the sensation of calm comes from an act of the mind, and is not just due to physical comfort of the body. Some degree of discomfort is also necessary to prevent one falling asleep. But beyond this I am unable to understand the great emphasis on correct posture. Perhaps there is something personal about this, as I am particularly stiff in the legs myself, and have no hope at all of squatting cross-legged on the floor in the lotus posture.

From talking of anxiety, I brought him to discuss the question of pain. Although anxiety could be controlled by meditation, he thought that any control of pain was much more difficult, and something that only the masters could achieve. I was then foolish enough to say something which spoilt it all. And as soon as I said it, I bit my lip, as I realized it was my own conceit which was talking. I told him that a limited control of pain was not all that difficult, as I myself had achieved it to the extent of having teeth extracted without discomfort. It is easy to drop a brick in conversation with Asians. This was one. Somehow as a result of my comment the poor man seemed to lose face; and our conversation never really regained its former spontaneity.

In Taipei I stayed in a beautiful new American-style hotel. It was just finished. Everything was new. There was only one problem. The staff did not know how to work it! It was as if people who had only seen ox-carts were suddenly given automobiles to drive. Even driving and operating a switchboard require some practice.

The hotel provided a little English-language newspaper. I well remember the first morning I saw it. I could hardly believe my eyes when I read the headline. 'China supports America in United Nations.' I had not seen a paper for a few days. Surely it could not be true! Then I laughed aloud as I realized what it was all about. In Taipei, Taiwan is China. Mainland China does not exist!

Encounter

I am sure it was just bad luck. I met people in Taiwan, but I made no real contacts. There are such differences in the way we meet people. So often we meet and talk. It goes all right

There is nothing wrong. We have our discussion and enjoy each other's company. But that is the end of it. There is no flare, no intensity, nothing which raises the meeting above the level of an everyday occurrence.

But just occasionally we meet someone, and the whole atmosphere is different. We get on together; we click; we are in 'cahoots'; we are 'en rapport'. When this occurs there is no mistaking it. These are very precious experiences, because they often have quite a profound and lasting effect on us. In existential philosophy, these meetings are known as 'encounters'.

An encounter does not seem to follow the logical laws of reason. It just happens. In a way, it is like love at first sight. But at the same time it is something different, as we can have encounters indiscriminately with people of our own sex, the opposite sex, with children and with old people.

In my own experience the effect of an encounter is always good and I believe this to be so with others. It seems that this form of contact with the other person somehow aids the integration of our personality, and as a result we feel better. More, we are better. Although these encounters may be quite brief, it seems to me that the contact with the other person is at a deeper level than usual. This is hard to explain. The subject-matter of the conversation is not necessarily deep. I feel that it is rather that the communication is between unconscious elements of the personalities of the two people. The words that we say, and the actions that we make, are merely the means by which this deeper understanding comes about.

Encounters occur in psychiatry, but only occasionally. I talk with my patients, and with nearly all of them I have good rapport; but this does not bring the interview up to the level of an encounter. When a true encounter takes place, I am immediately aware that the interview has been different. In such interviews it very often happens that little has been said either by me or the patient. When the patient goes, I am left with a sense of tranquillity; and on his next visit the patient almost invariably reports an improvement in his symptoms. But strangely enough subsequent interviews usually lack the quality that raises them to this level.

In my experience, encounters are rare in everyday life. But, with me, they seem to occur more often when I am travelling. This is one of the reasons why I enjoy travel so much. I often ask myself why this experience should occur more frequently under these circumstances. I do not know the answer. But a number of factors may come into it.

Encounters only occur when we leave ourselves unguarded. Thus they occur with those who are in love, and between doctor and patient in psychotherapy. On the other hand, with our friends we are unguarded in a slightly different way. We know that we can disclose confidences which will always be respected. Yet with our regular friends, good and trustworthy as they may be, there are usually limits to the extent we disclose our inner feelings. Perhaps I can express the idea more easily if I take a simple example. I talk with my psychiatrist friends at home, and we openly discuss the problems of our specialty, our successes and our failures. But sometimes when travelling I have met a psychiatrist for the first time, and this stranger has come to disclose even more than his problems, his successes and his failures. He has come to disclose, not so much what he thinks about the problems, but rather his own unformulated thoughts on the matter. 'Sometimes I have thought that the answer might be in this direction, but it seems silly as there is no evidence for it.' This is the type of disclosure that comes in an encounter, something deep down, personal, and something that our ordinary friends might ridicule. But this is disclosed to the chance acquaintance, the traveller, whom the other knows he may never see again. This is it. There is a security in these situations. It comes from a kind of anonymity which surrounds the traveller; and we unconsciously feel that we can test out our incompletely formulated ideas in a situation that does not really matter. In an unconscious way, the individual thinks, 'It can do me no harm even if this traveller does think I am crazy.' Whereas with our real friends we do not want to run the risk of appearing just a little ridiculous.

In travel there are tensions and relief from tension. Our fellow traveller who is suddenly relieved of tension may unburden himself to us, strangers as we are, in a way that would not happen in the routine of his daily life. Relief from tension of this nature may follow a stormy flight, failure of booking arrangements, problems with one's baggage or simply the escape from the difficulties of home or business. There is a sigh of relief; and if the person next to him is sympathetic, he unburdens himself of his anxieties in a way that may lead to an encounter between the two.

Then, of course, there is the feeling of community with one's fellow traveller. There are difficulties in common and shared experiences. Just as it is with lovers. Whether it is the beauty of a moonlight night or sexual intimacy, the shared experience is often an integral part of an encounter. In another way the same principles apply in psychiatry. In formal psychoanalysis the therapist is always a remote, enigmatic character, on quite a different plane to that of the patient. In these circumstances there is little possibility of an encounter. But in less formally structured psychotherapy in which the doctor to some extent shares the patient's experiences, an encounter may develop.

19 JAPAN

The Space Between

These few notes are really in the way of an addendum. Since submitting the manuscript of this little book for publication I I have been in Japan to attend another meeting on the medical use of hypnosis.

For a special lecture I was anxious to choose some topic which would appeal to our Japanese hosts. At first I could not think of anything suitable. Then I had a brain-wave, and hit upon 'The Space Between' as the title for my lecture. This is a well-known concept in Japanese art. It refers to the relationship of one object to another. By varying 'The Space Between' the objects themselves take on new meaning and new qualities, so that harmony is preserved in the work. 'The Space Between' comes to have significance in itself. There is meaning in absence as well as in presence. This is seen as a characteristic of Japanese painting, of the art of flower arrangement, of the ritual of the tea ceremony, of the arrangement of the stones in a Japanese garden. It is really a feature of Japanese life in general and is a recognized aspect of Zen Buddhism.

I applied these principles, which are so well known to the Japanese, to the art of hypnosis. This is a dynamic art. In it 'The Space Between' is ever changing as in the art of the lover. And as in the art of the lover, 'The Space Between' is used to convey all those things of the mind which are so basic to humanity that they cannot be expressed in mere words.

By using 'The Space Between' we can communicate with the patient. When he is afraid or uncertain we lessen 'The Space Between' us. He feels our support and is secure again. We use words, but we do not say very much. 'The Space Between' our words lengthens out. Silences come. They are easy, natural silences. We are relaxed, very relaxed. 'The Space Between' us becomes less and less. Our calm becomes his calm. It is all through him; and his mind slips back into a primitive mode of functioning in the way that is clinically known as hypnosis.

After the lecture, many of the Japanese came up to me and

began talking of Zen Buddhism. I had said nothing of Zen. But it was clear that the message had got through; and that I had been able to interpret a scientific procedure in terms of their basic philosophy. Somehow they came to look upon me as the Westerner who at least had made the attempt to see things with their eyes. But there was another side to this situation. There was a lot of talk about the relationship of Zen to psychiatry in general. The Americans were clearly out of their depth. They kept coming to me, two and three at a time, 'Just what is Zen? I have hardly heard of it. I can't understand it.'

But it was not all smooth sailing. Later at the conference I was chairman of a discussion panel on 'Hypnosis and Religion'. I gave a paper on 'Transcendental Religious Experience' in which I described experiences of prayer, possession, and natural awe in which a strange state of consciousness develops so that the individual is rather glassy eyed, ceases to think critically, and loses awareness of his immediate environment. I pointed out the similarity to hypnosis, and suggested that in both hypnosis and transcendental religious experience the mind made a regression to a simpler form of functioning. I said that I thought it likely that the same thing happened at the moment of 'sartori' or enlightenment in Zen practice. But when it came to the discussion, a professor of Zen Buddhism, who was on the panel with me, strongly disagreed, saying that regression had nothing to do with Zen. Then a well-known, old and respected exponent of Zen quickly rose in the audience supporting the professor. This type of reaction with open disagreement in public is unusual in Japan as it transgresses the principle of face-saving. However, more was to come, and worse. A younger Japanese on the panel got up, strongly supported my contention, and flatly disagreed with his two elders. Then it was on. Open frank discussion in the western style. Imagine my confusion. I was not only the centre of discussion, but was also chairman of the meeting. Speaker quickly followed speaker. The translators could not keep up on the simultaneous translating system. I did not know what was going on. Then everyone relaxed, and was happy, and thought the open discussion had all been very good. Next day people were still talking about it.

In a foreign culture with its own precise manners and customs one is always in danger of making a faux pas. The

Japanese president of the congress is a man whom I very greatly respect. He had achieved in his own person a very remarkable synthesis of two extremes, both of which I believe are essential to the true physician. He is an experimental investigator of the highest order. In this he is cold, detached, objective, in fact the real scientist. I feel quite sure that his work in this field will soon come to be widely quoted throughout the world. But there is another side to him, the philosophical side. I do not refer to his book-knowledge of Buddhism, but to his way of living it, as is shown by his humility, his compassion for his patients and his desire to understand their inner life. I had met his wife, but was unable to talk with her because of the language barrier. A little gift at the end of the conference would be a token communication. I did not know what to give. So I took a taxi to a florist shop. There were some beautiful red roses, just budding, and they had the longest stems I have ever seen on roses. I brought them to her hotel myself. I thought the man at the desk smiled rather strangely when I left them with him. Next day I casually mentioned the matter to a friend. Then half-memories of what I had read about giving gifts in Japan started to come back to me. Was it that lovers chose red flowers? And buds! Were they not particularly significant; and long stems too! I am still confused. This kind of thing happens all too easily in Japan.

The Sound of One Hand Clapping

Many of the papers at the meeting made reference to Zen practice, and there was a formal lecture on the subject by an expert. I was very disappointed in the lecturer as a person. To me he seemed a very aggressive man and lacking in any ordinary humility. I casually asked others about him, and they seemed to have the same impression. I felt on the brink of disillusionment.

I had heard of a large Zen temple which would sometimes accommodate western visitors for the purpose of study. I had written to the abbot asking if he would take me for a few days. I had no idea at all what to expect. I know that the Japanese are extremely cleanly people, but I had been warned that this does not always apply to the monks, who, as a part of the discipline of their life, use very little water, and in fact are often lousy. I do not know if this is true or not. But it seemed that I should take some precautions. A few days before leaving for Japan I was discussing this at home with my family. I was promptly advised that if I wanted to get some lice powder I should get it myself and not send the little girl from my professional rooms on such an errand. So I went to the pharmacist. There was a number of people in the shop. I thought I had better not whisper 'lice powder please'. That would surely make it worse. So I faced up to it, and said the awful words in a loud, firm voice. Then the panic thought came to me. 'He will think I want it for a dog and give me something too strong for my skin.' So, again in a firm voice, I clarified the situation, 'I want it for myself.' Psychiatrists speak of ideas of reference when an individual feels that people are looking at him in some strange way. This was my experience at that moment. Such are the problems of the amateur traveller. But I am happy to report that my precautions were quite unnecessary and the visitors' section where I was quartered could not have been cleaner.

I had good luck in the temple right from the start. There were three other Europeans, an American psychologist and his wife who was also a psychologist, and a Dutch woman doctor who spoke fluent English. By a strange coincidence the psychologist had heard me lecture in America a few years previously. This broke the ice, and they welcomed me into their little group. The three of them were serious students of Zen. The Americans were planning for two years' study, and the Dutch doctor had also spent some time in India studying yoga practice. We had long discussions into the night reminiscent of my student days.

On the evening of my first day they had been invited to another temple. Just once a year relatives and friends of the monks are allowed to visit. It was dusk when we arrived. We followed the sound of chanting through a beautiful moss garden. There, around the graves of bygone priests, the monks were chanting sutras from the ancient Vedanta. Relatives and friends stood nearby, about twenty of them. Their children played unconcerned among the graves. The droning incantation of the monks went on and on. It was calm beyond belief. Sounds were quietened by the blanket of garden moss. The air stirred and relieved the oppressive heat. The day was gone, finished. So much more was gone. I had no desire to move; I had no desire to think. It was experience beyond the logic of thought. Then it was finished. Each monk in turn went to the burning incense; bowed; and filed past where I was standing, looking neither to the right nor to the left.

Then we went to the zendo. This is the hall in which the monks live and meditate. Around the sides of the zendo there is a raised platform about six feet wide and two feet high. This is covered by the usual Japanese 'tatami' plaited rush floor covering. Each monk had one tatami strip six feet by three. In addition he has a little locker about one foot square. This is his home; his life for year after year. Here he meditates by day, and here he stretches out to sleep at night. On this day of the year the zendo is decorated with ingeniously contrived paper lanterns. There is an inner paper cylinder which is suspended so that it can rotate. Under it there is a lighted candle. The hot air from the candle rises and turns the cydinder as it comes through slots in the upper end. Pictures and designs are painted on the sides of the cylinder. This is suspended inside the square outer covering of the lantern which is made of translucent paper. The reflection of the paintings on the inner cylinder are thrown on to the outer square sides of the lantern, and slowly move across them as the paper cylinder rotates. It all has a child-like quality which is so consistent with the simplicity of the Zen way of life.

Back in our own temple we talked about it all. In Zen, two important ways to enlightenment are meditation and koan study. A koan is a problem which does not have a rational solution. This leads the mind beyond reason, to understanding, to enlightenment, and eventually to Buddhahood.

But to the Westerner, the sheer irrationality of it makes the koan appear as an insuperable problem. The Zen student must first learn to meditate. This involves the physical torture of sitting in the very uncomfortable lotus posture for long periods, and at the same time keeping the mind free. The preliminary mastering of meditation may take years. Then when this is accomplished the student is given a koan upon which to meditate. A common first koan is the sound of one hand clapping. The student has interviews with the master in which he reports progress. These interviews are known as sanzen. It may be a matter of years before the first koan is solved. The student is then given others.

All this seems irrational. Of course, this is just what is intended. The purpose is to free the mind. And one of the things from which it must be freed is the constricting tie of reason. The aim is something beyond the process of rationality, something that liberates the mind and allows understanding.

But is this altogether irrational? On the one hand it is not reasoned, but on the other hand it is not necessarily against reason. It is a system which works on a different plane from reason. And to come back to my study of hypnosis which brought me to these places, there is a clear similarity here. The patient in deep hypnosis sometimes gains understanding although nothing is said. This is not a process of reason, because the regression of hypnosis stills the logical functions of the mind. Rather the freedom from the constricting influence of reason has allowed free rein to our native intuition. The koan study of Zen would seem to be another path to the same end. But for me I think there are better ways than meditation on the sound of one hand clapping.

Human Sacrifice 1967

There was a lecture from one of the monks. This was to interested members of the Congress. About twenty western doctors attended. We were assembled in a temple and taken to a small hall which had one side open to a peaceful Japanese garden. We were then asked to sit on the floor in repose for half an hour, and then the monk would address us. I am sure that this appeared a ridiculous idea to my high pressure American colleagues. Here they were, in Japan for only a few days with so much to see, and they were asked to sit on the floor in repose for half an hour. I doubt if any of us attained much repose.

The monk spoke of the Buddha that lies dormant within us all. He talked of freeing the mind by meditation and the koans. And the more he talked the more I realized how impossible was his task. He was trying to explain something that aims to disregard the logical processes of the mind.

Any understanding of such a system requires something other than logical explanation. This is accepted by Zen practioners themselves who, unlike those of other Buddhist sects, pay relatively little attention to the great mass of Buddhist writing; and aim to gain their enlightenment through mental experience rather than by means of learning. Then I realized why he had wanted us to sit in repose. This was to have been some kind of little experience for us, something that might give us the feeling of what he was talking about. But even an experience simple as this requires some kind of preparation or explanation; and for this reason it failed.

He spoke of the analogy of the mirror. The mind must be as a mirror, and reflect the truth to us without distortion. To do this, the mind like the mirror must itself be blank. Such an idea fits in well with the psychoanalytic idea that when our inner conflicts are resolved the mind reflects reality without distortion.

In reply to a question as to how old he was when he first started Zen practice, he told us that he was the seventh child of poor parents and at the age of two and a half had been given to the monastery as a sacrifice. These were his words. In talking of it he did not seem particularly pleased. To what extent the sacrifice was motivated by the problems of the poor parents with a large family I do not know. I spoke to another monk who said he had come to the temple when he was ten. So the practice of sacrificing children cannot be too uncommon.

Breakfast with the Abbot

Living conditions in the visitors' quarters were not too uncomfortable. I soon became accustomed to going barefoot and sleeping on a thin mattress on the floor. But squatting on the floor remained a matter of great discomfort.

The first step in the practice of Zen is to learn to sit; and I never got to first base in this. I met a young American of twenty-nine who had had three years' arduous practice. He told me of the terrible agony that he had suffered in his legs during this period. The pain kept him awake at night. But it was getting less, and he was convinced that the end would be worth it all.

Each morning the four of us, the psychologist and his wife, the woman doctor and myself, had breakfast with the abbot. It was largely Japanese food, but as a courtesy to us Europeans it was served at a table. He spoke English, but not very well. I have been told that he is the only senior Zen practitioner in Japan who speaks English. This of course is one of the barriers to western understanding of the sect.

He was friendly and jovial; but conversation was always difficult. He held a kind of clinic at breakfast in which he explained to us some of the principles of Zen. I well remember my acute discomfort at these breakfasts. I was seated next to the abbot. I was very anxious to follow the complex matters which he was talking about. But if I listened to him my breakfast always slipped off my chopsticks. If I concentrated on my chopsticks I could not follow what he was saying. I was grateful for what little practice I had had. A few weeks before leaving for Japan I had bought some chopsticks, and much to the amusement of my family had insisted on eating in this fashion.

The abbot accepted me as serious in trying to find out something about Zen, and he arranged for me to meet the roshi. The roshi is the Zen-master, the spiritual leader of the particular temple group. It was an honour to be granted an interview, as it is very hard even for the monks to see the roshi. The abbot acted as interpreter as none of the roshis speak English.

I went half expecting to be disillusioned, as memories of the aggressive Zen professor at the Congress were still with me. But I could not have been more impressed. He was profoundly calm and at ease. He was intelligent, sensitive and gave the impression of great kindliness. Unlike the yogis who are detached and make no emotional response, he had a soft and easy smile which came with ease and naturalness. The muscles of his face were smoothed out as if reflecting the calm beneath. His eyelids were nearly closed and remained so during the interview even when he turned from me to the abbot, or when he smiled in response to some question. And I thought how slit eyes often make one suspicious of the individual. But there was none of that about this man; and the impression was that his eyelids were half closed because of the depth of repose within him. He seemed secure within himself and had no need for wide open eyes to be on the alert for danger.

I told him that I was a doctor, and that I was concerned about helping patients with pain and mental tension.

'Does Zen practice help a person to feel pain less?'

'No. It depends on the individual.'

'Does Zen practice help people to be less tense, less anxious?'

'No. It depends on the individual.'

He seemed to be denying the evidence before my eyes, that he was in fact one of the few serene people I have ever seen. But this is Zen. It states no objective. It claims no powers. I knew the traditional answer to the popular question. 'What is Zen?', so I did not ask it. The traditional answer is, 'Zen is nothing.'

A few days later I asked the American student, who had had three years' training in Zen, if he were less tense and anxious than before he started. He was absolutely definite that he was immeasurably more at ease. He felt that his threshold of perception of pain was much higher. He attributed this to his continued experience of pain in his legs in mastering the lotus squatting posture for meditation.

Under normal circumstances one would believe the master and disregard the student. But in this case I am inclined to do the reverse. Such is Zen, nothing but a paradox.

My life in the temple seemed to be a strange mixture of peace and turmoil. Sometimes at the early morning services held by the abbot the droning incantations would somehow bring out the wonder of it all; and I could sink into an attitude of mind in which I could accept the unknowable. There was a feeling of being part of it all, and I would drift into some state of consciousness in which there was a merging of identity with things around me. Then it would all be interrupted by the pain in my legs.

There were some quite wonderful moments when lying on the floor at night in my little room. I would hear the chanting in the middle of the night. The endless drone of it would barely intrude into the consciousness of my half-sleep. It was the sound of men in flight from the earthly to the mystical. And gongs would sound. And the reverberations would resound through the night. On and on. It was sound without end. And there was purity in the sound of it. And when I could hear it no longer, I knew that it still continued. And as dawn came, another sound blended into my sleep. It was repeated over and over again. Ooo, ooo, oo-oo. It was not until the next day that I realized that it was the cooing of doves. But it seemed part of it. And of course it was.

The American psychologist and his wife, the Dutch woman doctor and myself were soon a tightly knit group. This was good. In these strange surroundings there was a need to share things. It was not so much the physical strangeness of the things around us, but rather the other strangeness of the experiences within ourselves. It was not so much a matter of new thoughts, because thought belongs to the intellect, and we were not concerned with the intellect. Nor was it a matter of feelings, because they belong to the emotions and have no part in this life. They were moments of awareness of paralogical understanding. But words have no meaning in themselves; it is only the experience.

Non-duality, this was a recurring theme at the abbot's breakfast-time discussions. There is no body and mind; no then and now; no here and there. As long as we perceive things in this fashion, we are not free. Above this there is another system, another order of being. We were earnest in trying to understand, all four of us. Then someone would say, 'No, we must not try to understand for that is a function of the intellect'.

The American psychologist and his wife were both experienced in group therapy. This is a form of psychological treatment in which patients are seen in a group; they talk about their problems together, and react emotionally to each other. An important part of this treatment is clarifying the individual's inner motives. We were obviously such a group ourselves. The Americans were bent on analysing our own motives. Why had we come here? What were we seeking? Simple explanations were torn aside. It was no use saying, 'I came to see how Zen works', or 'I came to see if Zen helps people with anxiety and pain, so that I could use it with my patients.' No. There had to be something deeper, some need of our own personality that we were fulfilling in this strange search. I think this may well be so. But it is too close to the bone; and their insistent analysis of each other shattered the harmony of the group. No one was spared. I was older than they were, and I was better able to let these devastating analyses pass me by. But they could not do so. Sometimes they were on the verge of tears. There were bursts of silly and inappropriate laughter. There were tensions between husband and wife, who on occasion to relieve their own disquiet would start a relentless analysis of the other poor woman. It was clear to me that they were not gaining any understanding, but were set on a foolish course of self destruction. I have had psychology students and medical undergraduates as patients, who have been precipitated into severe nervous illness by this type of analytical discussion. But how could I help them? How could I stop them?

I knew that if I suggested that they should lay off this analysis of each other, the immediate reply would be, 'Oh, you are frightened of the truth.'

The hour of my departure was hastening on. I had an urgent feeling that there was something I should do; that there was something that I could do. But it had to be done at the right moment or everything would be worse. No logical explanations that would only be torn down, no further analysis that would only be analysed still further; yet I felt that some simple and appropriate act would crystallize calm and understanding from all the turmoil that was in them. I have seen this happen many times with patients. But the moment would not come. I made efforts to manipulate things. But no. Could I stay another day or two, and do this which should be done? No. Unlike the Zen monks, I was committed to reality as we know it. I felt that I was leaving with still unfinished business. They came to see me off at the porch. There were also the abbot's wife and a couple of young priests. It seemed to take me ages to get my shoes on. I turned and waved another goodbye. It was a long straight path from the porch to the gate, very long and very straight. Half way down the path I turned again. They were still there. I walked on. On my left, there was a high wall; on my right, was the temple garden. At the end of the path I turned again. They were still there. The scene remains fixed in my mind.

Then in the train I began to think about it all. I do not believe that I shall ever want to follow Zen. It seems to me that there must be some better way to understanding than meditation upon the irrational koan. I had really learned nothing from this experience. But at the same time I am aware that I have gained much from it. And this in itself is Zen.

When the Lights Faded

A few days after leaving the temple I was sitting in the great dining room of one of the leading hotels in Tokyo. I was by myself. I had just finished dinner, and was leisurely taking coffee. The band was playing softly, and couples were dancing on the floor. I was tired; and I let my mind drift into the meditative state which I had been studying in the temple. It all happened quite naturally and imperceptibly. My mind drifted with the music. The room was a great dark emptiness with the table lights making little spots of brightness. The shadowy waiters moved as ghost figures. The couples dancing on the floor were misty silhouettes. It was all quite wonderful. Then, as I came out of the meditative trance, what a contrast! The dancers were no longer misty shapes. The brightness of women's dresses almost startled me. In fact the whole room had a vividness of colour about it which had completely disappeared during my meditation. Then it came to me. In the meditative trance I had lost my colour vision. I repeated the experience, this time looking out through the window at all the bright, coloured lights of the Ginza district. As I let myself go, the colour of the spectacle faded, and I found myself gazing at a myriad spots of uncoloured light.

Perhaps this does not seem very important to the reader. But here again was further evidence for my theory that meditation involves mental regression. In the great march of evolution, when living things first began to see, we must assume that these first glimpses of the world were in the very simple vision of black and white, or perhaps rather in shades of grey. Then all the complexity of colour vision developed with the process of further evolution.

Now, what had I done in the hotel dining-room? Surely I had let my mind slip back to a more primitive way of functioning. This is just what I had been postulating only a few weeks previously at the medical meeting. And as far as I know this evidence, which is so extremely simple in itself, has never previously been reported in the scientific writing on such matters.

And I thought more about this simple observation. The same principle must surely apply to other sensations. And to pain itself. I felt that I could now better understand the problem of pain, which had brought me to venture into these strange places. The sensation of pain, like the sensation of sight, must have grown in complexity over the period of evolution. This is what we would expect. Pain that becomes agony, or is associated with anguish or even anxiety must be a sensation which belongs to man and which lower animals are spared. In the regression of hypnosis the mind goes back and functions at a primitive level so that the colour, as it were, goes out of the sensation of pain. As a result pain loses its hurt. And this of course is how I came to have my teeth extracted without discomfort and without calling upon the mechanisms of suggestion or dissociation which are usually employed in hypnosis.

It is what we do in Japan.

Shinto was the indigenous religion of the Japanese before the advent of the Buddhist, Confucian and Taoist doctrines from mainland China. It is a simple primitive faith; and in its pure form this simplicity lends both beauty and wonder. It all concerns the Kami. These are the spirits, the powers and the influences which are all about us affecting our everyday life. Most natural phenomena have their Kami. Thus there are spirits of growth and fertility, of streams and mountains, and most important, spirits of ancestors.

This was a delightfully simple way of understanding that which cannot be understood. As one would expect, small shrines were built where special Kami could be worshipped. Later there came great shrines, where priests invented special ways for calling upon the spirits. So there developed the magic symbolism and ritual which is such a part of Shinto in the present day. At the same time Shinto came to form a peaceful co-existence with Japanese Buddhism. This of course is a feature of the religious life of Japan today, so that Japanese Buddhists commonly have a little Shinto shrine in their home. They may be married according to Shinto rites, but on death have a Buddhist funeral. This same happy integration of the two faiths is seen in the temples and shrines themselves, as in each we see symbols of the other faith. A further influence has been the growth in the importance of the spirits of the ancestors. This developed into the national religion of State Shinto centring around the worship of the spirits of the ancestors of the Emperor.

I was at Nikko trying to find out something of the strange symbolism of Shinto. The shrine, set in a grove of ancient trees, must surely be one of the most beautiful places of religious worship. To avoid the main stream of pilgrims and tourists I went there early in the morning. I thought I might find some guide or English-speaking priest who could help me. But no. However I picked up with a student. He was well enducated, had travelled in Europe and was eager to be helpful. I asked him the meaning of the various symbols. He did not know, but he would find out for me. He asked other pilgrims. But they did not know. Then some attendants, then a priest. He came back shaking his head, and said, 'It is just the way we have in Japan.'

This of course is the ultimate answer to so many things.

In most Shinto shrines and many Buddhist temples there is a system of telling fortunes. There is a small fee, and one takes a slip of paper. I showed mine to the student to translate. 'The more one gets fame, the more the soul is modest.' In most shrines the slip of paper is folded and tied to a special tree, so that the spirits will see it. Many such trees have thousands of these strips of paper tied to them.

When making an offering, it is important to call the attention of the spirits. One throws the coin into the offering box from a little distance, bows twice, then claps twice with the hands, and bows once again. But the idea of calling the attention of the gods is not confined to Shinto. I remember a few years ago in Nepal I had toiled up to a rather remote temple on a hill-top. The temple was still and almost deserted. There was the place to make the offering, and near at hand sat a priest, impassive, inscrutable and apparently quite unaware of my standing in front of him. I remember admiring the huge bronze bell at his side. It was fully six feet tall, and by it there was a great log of wood suspended horizontally by ropes so that it could be used to strike the bell. With little thought as to the purpose of all this, I dropped a coin through the wooden slots of the receptacle. Then, boom. I nearly jumped out of my skin. And the ring of it went on and on, echoing through the mountains. Not only the gods knew of my offering, but so did everyone about, even those in the village in the valley. I felt my miserable offering should have been ten times, a hundred times greater. And still the echoes of it went on. Then at last there was quiet again. Next day, in the village below, when I heard the sound of the distant gong, I knew what it was all about.

To Make the Mind Empty

In an American journal of hypnosis I had read an article about Shamanism by a Korean doctor. I wrote to the author explaining my interest in such matters, and arranged to visit him in Korea on my way home from Japan.

Shamanism is an ancient secret cult which uses both magic and trance. It probably had its origin in Russia, and spread to small groups in the Far East and Middle East. In Korea the Shamans are mainly women. In fact they are witches. Their practices are very secret. Sometimes they are called upon to help the sick. There are preliminary rituals and chanting. The Shaman goes into a trance holding a stick in her hand. Then her trance deepens. If the stick in her hand points upwards the patient will get better, but if it points downwards the sick one will surely die. The Shaman's power of suggestion is so great that the patient follows the fateful prognostic sign of the stick. If the patient has some serious organic illness he obtains some temporary relief as a result of suggestion which is regarded as proof of the Shaman's power; then if he relapses it is considered to be due to some other influence.

I was taken to meet a woman professor of Buddhism at the university, and I had some long discussions with her. She was an easy and natural woman of middle age. I think she was perhaps greater as a scholar of Buddhist philosophy than as a participant in Buddhist practices such as the monks I had seen in the temples where I had stayed in Japan. Strangely enough her father had been a Christian pastor. She herself had practised Buddhism for twenty years, meditating for an hour in the morning and three hours at night, combining this with her duties as wife and professor.

There was no doubt in her mind that Buddhism had brought calm to her mind, and had given her an ability to cope with pain and discomfort.

She seemed to me to be a kind of practical Buddhist, and in a way had attained the best of both worlds, both that of material reality and that of the inner spirit.

She was practical too in her answers to my questions. I asked her about the importance of the cross-legged lotus posture for meditation. Unlike most other authorities whom I have asked she said the lotus posture was not all that important, as meditation was essentially a matter of the mind. She thought that Europeans like myself could meditate best in a sitting position provided that the back was straight and the head erect so that there was a minimum of tension in the muscles. This seemed to make sense to me.

She explained that the essential thing in meditation is emptiness of the mind. When the mind is empty, wisdom comes. She laid great emphasis on this state of emptiness of the mind. It is clearly different from our common ideas of thinking of nothing or making the mind go blank. It seems that both these ideas involve activity of the mind, and this is not a part of the particular mental state which she was describing.

The whole theme of what she was saying seemed to fit in with my own ideas about hypnosis. I believe that in hypnosis the mind does sometimes empty itself of all logical thought. In this state the patient's problems are sometimes solved. I believe that this happens as a result of paralogical intuitive activity of the mind which is normally inhibited by the logical functions of the intellect. She expressed the same idea, only more aptly and simply. When the mind is truly empty, wisdom comes.

We talked of many things, and I am afraid I questioned her rather relentlessly. I was asking her about the incantation of the priests at Buddhist services. These incantations are usually in classical Chinese, a language which is not understood by the people of Korea or Japan. In fact the intonation is such that it would be impossible to understand the words even if one were familiar with the language. The situation is exactly similar to that of many Christian services which are held in Latin. She agreed with me that not being able to understand the logical content of the service helped towards this emptiness of the mind which she stressed as so important.

All this made me think of a Buddhist service which I had attended in Japan a few weeks previously. At this service there had been endless, droning incantation accompanied by clapping together of two small pieces of wood. As is usual, the priests clapped wooden pieces, but in this sect all the worshippers have their own pieces of wood. The clapping was almost deafening. The rate of the clapping was very fast, about twice the rate of the normal heart beat. In this particular service, I am sure that half the worshippers were in a deep trance. Thus the monotonous incantation and the clapping had facilitated the state of emptiness of the mind which my friend stresses as so important. She emphasized that Buddhism, unlike Christianity, provided different paths for different people to the same goal. Thus the path of Zen with its abstruse concepts could only be the path for the few, the intelligent and scholarly.

Kwan Yin

Since I first started to write about these experiences, I have wanted to say something about Kwan Yin. But somehow it has seemed too difficult. I think I have fallen in love with her, and that of course makes it hard.

It must have been on my first visit to Hong Kong. In a curio shop I found a beautiful stone figure. This was some time ago, and then I did not even know the name of the lady who has come to steal my fancy so completely. She was standing at ease, about two feet high, clad in the flowing drapes of the classical Chinese, and with that mystique of expression which communicates the indefinable. I knew I had to have her. I bargained and bought her. And since then she has stood on the bookshelves in my study.

When one falls for a girl, a single picture is never enough. On my next visit to Hong Kong I spent the whole of my time in search of another. Do not be mistaken. Do not think of the hundreds of factory made figures of Kwan Yin with which the shops abound. No. My lady is not like those. The fact remains that each time I have been to Hong Kong I have come home with a stone figure of my lady. It has become a family joke.

One of the strange things about her is that she was originally a man. He was a Bodisatva, one who has attained Buddhahood, a kind of saint; and his saintliness was concerned with the depth of his compassion. Bodisatvas are always rather sexless. Perhaps all that is spiritual within them leads to something beyond sex. Then with the spread of Buddhism from India to China, Kwan Yin became worshipped as a female deity. It may be that compassion is an attribute of woman rather than of man. People think of her as the taking-away-fear Buddha. To Europeans she is known as the Goddess of Mercy. I know nothing of China, but I have seen her worshipped widely by Mahayana Buddhists in Hong Kong, Taiwan and Japan.

I have found my stone image brings with it a sense of beauty and repose. But more than this, there is such a sense of mystique that it seems to have captivated me. So I continue my search for another. I have searched around the dust of old shops in narrow streets where such things are sometimes found. I have sought her from lush curio shops of the great hotels, where the Rolls-Royce and the rickshaw wait outside. One very hot day there was an old rickshaw-man squatting on the foot-board of his rickshaw as is their custom while waiting for a passenger. He was very old. He was half asleep, half in a stupor. He was a worn-out man; his body almost gone, his mind insensitive to the noise and bustle that was all about him. I had just bought half a dozen mandarins to take to my hotel room. I quietly put one by his side, but he awoke from his stupor, and his eyes looked at me. Then arms stretched out from all directions, and I had to be off. Then, by strange coincidence, twice in the next few days I saw an old rickshaw-man wave to me. It was he again, not asking for more, but still bowing his thanks. And he seemed stronger. Strength that could not have come from my miserable mandarin.

In my search I have passed women in the briefest mini skirts I have ever seen, women in the traditional garb of the Chinese, women in rags, women like Chinese film stars with neat dresses and trim figures. And women with chubby babies strapped to their backs, and women with emaciated children begging for a few cents. I have been to shops where they would discuss nothing until I was seated on a china stool, and had had a cup of green tea. In others they cared little if I came or went, and in some their anxiety to sell me something spoke of their need of basic necessities. A thousand times I have asked, 'Kwan Yin, Kwan Yin'. But they could not understand my pronunciation. 'Goddess of Mercy'. But they could speak no English. So I have rummaged around their shops. I have examined hundreds of stone figures of Kwan Yin, but none has had the strange quality of the first one which I so happily stumbled on.

I have sought her through all the turmoil that makes Hong Kong one of the most fascinating cities of the world. Through the bustle of it all; but no jostling, no pushing, that is not the way of the Chinese. Through the smell of narrow streets where the stench of it would be enough to stop my breathing. Passed beggars who made worse their deformities; and those who sat in the gutter quietly awaiting death to take them

Passed old men who looked as if they knew what it was all about; passed women whose gaunt eyes told that they had learned to accept what it was. Stepping over gutters of filth and children. Passed police whose impassive calm and efficiency makes them some of the finest in the world. Groups of jabbering tourists on their world cruise bent on buying junk from the Kowloon factories. Children playing in the streets whose widest horizon is the gutter of the next alley. And through all this nobody interferes. And it goes on late into the night. Women and girls come who would lead me to another love, but my desire is elsewhere.

And now I have several stone figures of my lady-love. They are all different, each reflecting the craftsman's own idea of the nebulous quality which finds expression in the concept of Kwan Yin. But as in life, none has the same mystique as the one which first so captivated my fancy.

Apologia

I have just read the manuscript. I started off with the idea of writing about some of the strange places that I have visited on my way from Australia to various medical meetings in America and Europe. But now I see that I have not done this. I have written mainly about myself; not the people and the places, but how I have reacted to them. I am sorry for this, for there are many wonderful sights for the visitor to see in these strange places.

But maybe there is another way of looking at it all. In strange places we see things differently. And perhaps it is that in strange places we can see ourselves differently too. And this may be just as wondrous as the new sights that are all around us when we travel. Some say that travel broadens the mind. Maybe that it deepens it too. If you can feel this, as I do, then I am glad I have written this little book.